Cynthia has a winner here!

We learn from reading *Ice Cream & Pretzels* that life writes its own script, often with surprising twists unpredicted and undesired. In this book, Cynthia records life up, down, and sideways. She covers parents, spouses, children, friends, relationships, and human needs. This series of essays is an easy read and actually educational, as they reveal not only the learning of life, but human and religious influences. These reflections on birth, life, and death are universal.

As you read this book, you will be making comparisons to your own life history.

William T. Delamar, author of
The Caretakers, Patients in Purgatory, The Hidden Congregation,
and *The Brother Voice*

Sept. 22, 2018

Querida Roberta,
Tell your stories!
No one else can.
Abrazos,
Cynthia

Ice Cream & Pretzels

and
Other
Stories

A Memoir
by
Cynthia
Claus

Ice Cream & Pretzels

and Other Stories

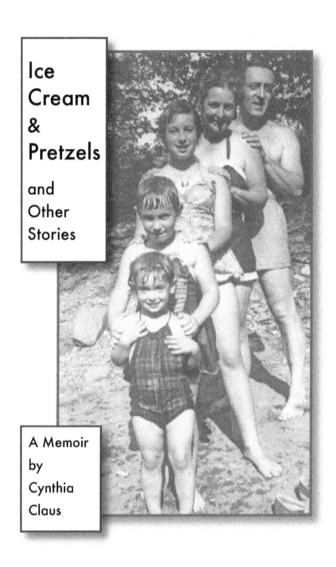

A Memoir by Cynthia Claus

PASHMINA PRESS

Printed in United States of America

First Printing, 2018

ISBN-13: 978-1986398596

ISBN-10: 1986398595

Pashmina Press

751 N. Taylor St.

Philadelphia, Pa. 19130, USA

www.cynthiaclaus.com

10 9 8 7 6 5 4 3 2 1

Cover photo:
The Claus family, circa 1955. From top:
Anton, Eleanor, Cynthia, Julia, and Gretchen

Frontispiece photo:
The Claus family, in 1961 or '62, on board ship
prior to Anton and Eleanor's departure for Europe.

Opposite title page:
The three Claus girls, 1965.

Dedication

To those who have passed through my life
and added to it in some important way—
parents, sisters, grandparents, children, grandchildren,
teachers, Sunday School teachers, friends, neighbors,
work colleagues, therapists, housekeepers—
I am who I am today because of being raised in my particular
family and being touched by all of you.
And to those of you still in my life
and those I have yet to encounter—
thank you for accompanying me
on this splendid, amazing journey.

About This Book

In a series of candid vignettes and one poem, Cynthia takes us into her family of origin to revisit her physician parents, whose lives were impacted in unexpected, far-reaching ways by her father's service in World War II, and into her life with them and her two younger sisters, covering several decades. We meet grandparents, lifelong friends, and mother substitutes. Dark family secrets are revealed. Questions are raised. Other tales explore Cynthia's work history in such divergent places as her father's medical office and a seminary. We are with her during the dissolution of two marriages and a nostalgic look back at a high school romance. Always honest, Cynthia tells it like it was—the good, the bad, and the very bad—with feeling and understanding, and eventually forgiveness.

Introduction

*Truth has a voice.**

As I prepared this book for publication, I was struck by the difference between how my family members appear in the photos in this book with what is divulged in the stories. It reminded me of a report I once heard on NPR about a study of family photo albums around the world. The conclusion drawn by the study, after interviewing the families who owned the albums, was that universally, families wanted to show through their photos that "We were happy and we loved each other." My photos seem to say that, also, and indeed, no matter what else was going on, I did know that I was loved.

As is often said, "Nobody writes about his or her idyllic childhood." I would be the first to admit that my upbringing was certainly not all bad, and many, many children had it so much worse than I did. I've read the memoirs to prove it. But much of it was very bad. I certainly learned what not to do as a parent, and I could hardly wait to be one so that I could put into practice what I thought were better methods of child-rearing.

A podcast for memoirists that I listened to recently cautioned about the difference between "writing for therapy" and writing a coherent memoir around a theme. While I am sure that I gained much relief and release by writing these stories over many years, which could be characterized as therapeutic, I hope my readers will find some elements of their own lives reflected in mine, and can learn from the stories that life goes on, that we can overcome our beginnings and work to correct and not repeat them, that we don't need to wind up in the same place that we started, and that we can finally arrive at forgiveness.

Most of these stories were written in a unique writing class, Essentially English, which I attended over several years at my children's school, Germantown Friends in Philadelphia, while they were students there and for years after. The choices of English classes of the juniors and seniors were opened up not only to the students, but to their parents, neighbors of the school, and, indeed, to the general public. The offerings included poetry, movie watching and critiquing, short story reading, the reading of novels, and writing of all kinds, including the one I was interested in, memoir.

The classes were held at the school in the evening once a week for three hours. While initially the students and the adults sat in separate clumps around the huge table, the teachers always matched a younger person with an older one when it came time to read the stories we had written, so that soon the ice was broken and there was good exchange and warmth between the two groups.

We were given weekly prompts, and I don't remember a time when anyone—student or adult—came to class without something he or she had written. In addition to the sharing of stories across the generation gap, people could volunteer to read their stories to the whole class. At the end of each class, the teacher collected the assignments and returned them the following week, covered with suggestions and comments. I took other writing classes in other settings, always in memoir, but the details of those have faded.

In other years I was invited to join a group of very serious writers, some published, which also met weekly. In all of these writing situations, while I wrote my heart out, I never thought of myself nor referred to myself as a writer. But with the publication of my first book in July 2017, *An Orchid Sari: The Personal Diary of an American Mom in 1960s India,* I felt that I could honestly call myself a writer.

Because my parents were both osteopathic physicians, a somewhat-unknown and often-misunderstood medical practice that is alluded to in these stories, I thought a short explanation was in order. And what better place to turn for this but to the American Osteopathic Association's (AOA) website:

"What is a DO?

"Doctors of Osteopathic Medicine, or DOs, are fully licensed physicians who practice in all areas of medicine. Emphasizing a whole-person approach to treatment and care, DOs are trained to listen and partner with their patients to help them get healthy and stay well.

"DOs receive special training in the musculoskeletal system, your body's interconnected system of nerves, muscles and bones. By combining this knowledge with the latest advances in medical technology, they offer patients the most comprehensive care available in medicine today.

"Osteopathic physicians focus on prevention, tuning into how a patient's lifestyle and environment can impact their wellbeing. DOs strive to help you be truly healthy in mind, body and spirit—not just free of symptoms."

And because my religion, Unitarian Universalism, is also unfamiliar to many, I studied the Unitarian Universalist Association (UUA) website for help in interpreting it for a wide audience.

While Unitarian Universalism has a rich history starting in Europe in the 16th century with the rejection of the trinity and of mainstream Christianity's concept of eternal damnation, I will concentrate here on what UUism is now in the United States. Today, UU congregations are non-creedal, diverse, and inclusive of many beliefs. We are led by Seven Principles, which we hold as strong values and moral guides:

1st Principle—The inherent dignity and worth of every person;

2nd Principle—Justice, equity, and compassion in human relations;

3rd Principle—Acceptance of one another and encouragement to spiritual growth in our congregations;

4th Principle—A free and responsible search for truth and meaning;

5th Principle—The right of conscience and the use of the democratic process within our congregations and in society at large;

6th Principle—The goal of world community with peace, liberty, and justice for all;

7th Principle—Respect for the interdependent web of all existence of which we are a part.

We live out these principles in a "living tradition" of inspirational wisdom and spirit, drawn from sources as diverse as wisdom from the world's religions, Jewish and Christian teachings, humanist teachings, spiritual teachings of Earth-centered traditions, words and deeds of prophetic men and women, and direct personal experience.

When we read scripture, regardless of the religious tradition from which it comes, we interpret it as a product of its time and place. In our tradition, scripture is never the only word nor the final word.

We join together not because we have a shared concept of the divine. UUs are agnostic, theist, atheist, and everything in between. A popular saying among UUs is that "We don't need to think alike to love alike." UU beliefs concerning life after death are informed by both science and spiritual traditions; most UUs live with the assumption that life does not continue after death, but rather we work to make this life, now, here on earth the very best that it can be for everyone. Service is our sacrament. And we strive to do this in "beloved community" open to all, regardless of race, color, nationality, sexual orientation, or identification.

One thing that I regret, which I realized while amassing these stories, is that neither of my parents ever spoke to us about their lives as children or about their parents. This has left a big hole in my understanding of them as people and as my parents. I hope that the combination of what I've told my children over the years about my upbringing and what is revealed in these stories will help to fill in any gaps that remain in their understanding of me.

* Rev. Dr. Gregory Seltz, *The Lutheran Hour, July 13, 2014*

ICE CREAM
& PRETZELS
and Other Stories

Stories have to be told or they die, and when they die, we can't remember who we are or why we're here.

–*Sue Monk Kidd*

List of Stories

A Memory of Barbara

I was 12 that night when Barbara slept over at my house. The visit itself wasn't unusual; Barbara and I often stayed at each other's homes. Our parents, or at least our fathers, were very good friends, and through family get-togethers Barbara and I became best friends.

Barbara and her older brother, Jim, on whom I had a crush, and their parents, Bob and Mae, were patients of my father's. Which came first—patient or friend—I don't know. A skilled machinist, Bob was in a far different line of work compared to the other friends of my physician parents, so I'm not sure how they would have met. And Barbara's family was not from our Philadelphia neighborhood, where most of those in my father's general practice lived (my mother was no longer practicing medicine by this time). Yet our fathers had a unique friendship that spanned many years. They loved to play poker with other male friends, and the whole family visited us on some summer weekends at our cabin on Analomink Lake in the Pennsylvania Pocono Mountains.

On one of those Poconos visits, Jim, Barbara, and I played games of strip Fish in the rowboat, since we didn't know how to play poker, staying down at the end of the lake where no one could see us. Of course we never went too far in the undressing, just enough to be titillating. Another time Barbara and I were spying on Jim, who was out on the lake fishing, and I hid myself behind a huge rock on the shoreline. I stepped directly onto a wasps' nest, and immediately ran screaming toward the house followed by a long, thick column of angry wasps. My father met me at the screen door to the porch but wouldn't allow me into the house. He kept shouting, "Go into the lake! Go into the lake!" I spun around and ran back down the hill out onto our dock, threw myself into the water in my clothes and shoes, still screaming, and immersed myself until the wasps dispersed, coming up occasionally for quick gasps of air. The cool water helped calm the pain of my many, many wasp stings.

Throughout all our times together, Barbara's mom seemed very glamorous to me. She was a Marilyn Monroe look-alike, except with dark hair. She polished her fingernails and toenails, something my own mother never did. But Mae developed cancer and had to have a double mastectomy. She was the first woman I'd ever known to have her breasts removed. It was a frightening thing for me.

Mae never really got better after the surgery. The doctors weren't able to get all the cancer, and it had invaded her organs. She'd been very sick for a long time. My father, as her primary physician and a dear family friend, had been visiting her daily in the hospital, now that the end seemed to be near.

As Barbara and I slept in the double bed in my third-floor bedroom, I was awakened early to hear my father climbing the stairs wearily. I watched in silence as he walked to a window and lifted the shade to let in the weak early-morning light.

By now both Barbara and I were fully awake but still quiet. I propped myself up on my elbow as my father opened the other shade. He was dressed impeccably in a suit, but he looked awful; he needed a shave. He slowly walked to Barbara's side of the bed, sat down, and put his hand on her blanket-covered shoulder.

"She's gone, Barbie," he said softly. "She died about an hour ago. She went in her sleep, peacefully. Your dad was there with her. He's still at the hospital, making arrangements." He gathered her up in his arms and rocked her gently as she began to cry. Then he included me in the hug and we all cried and rocked.

After a long while, he lowered us onto the bed and said he'd be back to check on us later. I was alone with my friend. It was my first experience with death and grief.

Barbara's crying ebbed and flowed, sometimes becoming a wail, other times just soft heaving. I held her and held her but didn't say much. I cried a lot, too. My pillow became uncomfortably wet. We lay in that bed all day, Barbara crying and I being there with her.

My parents came up occasionally one by one to sit on the bed and talk or to try to get us to drink some juice, but we just lay there, crying. Barbara's father finally came for her around four in the afternoon. I don't know where Jim was all this time.

I was really hungry by then, and in spite of what I'd gone through that day, I ate a big dinner. We talked about Mae as we ate.

23

Soon after that, the relationship between my family and Barbara's changed, especially when Bob moved the family to another state. Barbara and I exchanged letters for a long time, always promising to visit each other, but that never happened. The letters eventually got further and further apart and then stopped. Gradual goodbyes might be easier, but they are still goodbyes, and are still sad.

Date unknown

Ice Cream and Pretzels

My parents were of different religions, Mother a second-generation Unitarian and Daddy the same lineage Lutheran, both active participants in their respective Philadelphia congregations. They were married in my mother's living room by her Unitarian minister. But when the children started coming, a Solomonic decision was made for determining their religious training: the first child would go with my mother, the second with my father, and so on back and forth. This probably would have worked to everyone's satisfaction had we been an even number of children. Initially the third child went

25

to my mother's religion according to the plan. Although Gretchen started out going to Sunday school with me, somehow my father "got" her and she wound up at the Lutheran church for her religious upbringing.

On the Sabbath, Daddy and my two younger sisters, Julia and Gretchen, would go to Chestnut Hill to pick up my paternal grandmother, Grossmama, and would proceed to Reformation Lutheran Church in the West Oak Lane neighborhood. Mother and I would collect my maternal grandmother, Gramma, a few blocks from us in Mt. Airy, and go together to the Unitarian Society of Germantown.

My father, not content to have the score be two to one, would make me attend the Good Friday service at the Lutheran church. (There were no Unitarian services that day.) The Lutherans' service was designed in segments spanning three afternoon hours so people could come and go, staying as long as they liked. I was off from school the whole day and was directed to put in an appearance during one of the three hours. I always considered it a pain to leave whatever I was involved in midday, work or play, change into good clothes (we did the whole bit then—hat, gloves) and walk a mile or so to church, then return home and put my other clothes back on. I can't remember much about those services except that the segments dealt with the seven last words of Jesus. But because of that ritual and other times I attended services with Dad, I got to know the liturgy and the hymns pretty well.

My father must have "gotten" me a few other times, too, because when I attended a Lutheran chapel service at my place of employment decades later, I found that I knew all the words to the various recited creeds and prayers, and the sung and spoken responses as part of the liturgy. Just as I was the only holdout during Communion at that service, so I vaguely remember standing up with all the others at Reformation but remaining silent as they recited something in unison. I sometimes mouthed the words so as not to stand out as a nonbeliever in the crowd.

I would not take Communion at the Good Friday services either. Secretly, I was dying to try it. But I knew that it was not something to be taken lightly, for the experience. My sisters had to go to classes on weekday afternoons after school in preparation. Quite a fuss was made when they took Communion for the first time—new clothes, definitely.

Then they were confirmed, wearing beautiful white dresses and white Mary Janes. Each had a big lawn party at our house after her ceremony. There were gifts, also. Of course, they had to endure a year of preparation for that event, and the gifts tended to be of the Bible/cross on a chain/inspirational book sort, so perhaps I'm not envious after all.

I can remember vividly only two years of my early Unitarian religious training. The first was the curriculum titled "The Church Across the Street" around the sixth grade. About once a month, following several weeks of study about the religion, we would visit a different house of worship and get a sort of backstage tour by the minister, rabbi, or priest of that congregation. We could ask questions about the service in which we'd just participated or about the religious beliefs of the denomination that we had studied. As part of that course, we visited a synagogue during Succoth. The rabbi took us outside to see the congregation's sukkah. It was a sunny, warm fall day and the sukkah was appealingly decorated with fresh fruits and vegetables.

The other year I recall was LRY—Liberal Religious Youth. I was a teenager then and we met on Sunday evenings. We had discussions, planned conferences with other LRY groups, ate refreshments, played games, danced, and flirted a lot.

On Easter morning, Daddy would greet each of us as we came down for breakfast with a rousing "Christ is risen. Hallelujah!" I would have to respond, "Yes, Christ is risen. Hallelujah." And speaking of hallelujah, my father was a member of the choir at his church. They often performed the "Hallelujah" chorus from Handel's *Messiah*. Daddy would regale us with his version of it, with him singing the various parts, switching from his role as tenor up into a falsetto doing the soprano part and down into the bass range. To this day, I can do a pitch-perfect copy of that performance. It gave me the tiniest insight into my father's religion: he didn't take it all that seriously.

Going to church in those days meant dressing in our finest clothes. My grandmothers doted on us three sisters and competed with each other to dress us. (I think of them now as the Dueling Grandmothers.) Our clothes for Easter were especially grand. We'd be outfitted from head to toe each year: a pastel light wool spring coat, a new dress, an Easter bonnet, of course, white gloves, new shoes, and a matching purse. And while all this finery and the Easter baskets laden with chocolates and jelly beans, and the dyeing, hiding, and finding of eggs were thrilling and fun, what I really liked about Easter was that it signaled the beginning of our ice cream lunches after church.

On the drive home, Mother, Gramma, and I always stopped at Bredenbeck's, an old, traditional neighborhood bakery and ice cream parlor, and my mother ran in for the Sunday newspaper and several flavors of hand-dipped ice cream. Peach, chocolate, and coffee were favorites, particularly peach. We rushed the ice cream home to Gramma's; laid out spoons, napkins, and big, deep soup bowls on her breakfast room table, which overlooked her large garden; and tucked into mounds of ice cream with gusto. And we always had thick pretzel sticks with the ice cream, a Philadelphia tradition. Fresh, crisp, salty pretzel sticks. I frequently used my pretzel stick as a spoon to move the sweet treat from the dish to my mouth, and I was allowed to do this!

We three generations of females talked and laughed and ate ice cream with abandon. My mother and grandmother had several cups of coffee, which they sipped from delicate Rosenthal Bavaria china cups. When I finished my ice cream, I went into the yard. I longed to climb the peach tree—whose branches in the summer, laden with fruit, hung very low and had to be held up with tall wooden poles usually used to support a clothesline—but I couldn't in my Sunday clothes. Also in the summer, hundreds of yellow roses grew on latticework on the side wall of Gramma's garage. Soft green grass covered the expansive yard, and birds and warm, gentle breezes made sweet music on those carefree afternoons. I don't know what my father, Grossmama, and my sisters did about lunch on Sundays because I was with the ice cream-eating Unitarians.

I like to think that my mother and her mother were re-creating, if for only a couple of hours each week, what they had together earlier in life: just each other. My maternal grandfather died when my mother was only 16; he had been quite a bit older than Gramma. And my father had been in World War II and away for many years during my infancy and toddler years, so Mother and I lived with Gramma in her house during that time. I think they gave each other some of what they couldn't get from their spouses, one because of death, the other because of distance, both geographical and emotional. And I was just icing on their cake, the beloved first child, a smart, well-behaved daughter, and they poured their collective love onto me.

We three ate lunch together after church every week throughout the year, but for the life of me, I can't remember any of the lunches we shared at Gramma's when the weather was cold. It was the indulgence of the ice cream, the almost forbidden fruit, and the company of the women most important in my life that I cherish so vividly.

The interesting outcome of our different religious affiliations is that I, the Unitarian, am the only one of us three sisters who is involved with organized religion in any way. Some years before Mother died, my parents moved to Lebanon County, Pennsylvania, from the home where I grew up in Philadelphia, and she had either not found another Unitarian church to join or simply didn't care about it anymore. When my mother died, Daddy just called in the minister from the closest church, Methodist I think it was, who conducted a pretty nondenominational service in a funeral parlor.

When my father died seven years later, I had a memorial service in the chapel at my church. It was a Unitarian service through and through, but I asked my minister to acknowledge publicly Daddy's Lutheran heritage.

Since very few things are accidents in this life, I believe that the most telling fact about this somewhat unorthodox religious division in my family is how it played out in my adult life. While I am a very active member of the Unitarian church, I worked at The Lutheran Theological Seminary at Philadelphia for 13 years. I kept a foot in the religions of both parents, still doing the delicate dance required to navigate between them.

2005

My maternal grandmother, Florence Bell Boal, "Gramma" to me.

My mother, Eleanor Boal Claus, 1960.

33

Left on the Bus

The war kept my father away from home for the first three years of my life, and after he returned, my mother suffered a number of miscarriages. When their second child arrived, six years after me, I was already riding the L bus back and forth from my home in Mt. Airy to first grade at John Story Jenks Elementary School in Chestnut Hill, the neighborhood north of ours. This was not the elementary school that my home address would have dictated I attend, but I think now that Emlen, the school in my immediate neighborhood, was perceived as inferior to the school in upper-class Chestnut Hill, so my parents pulled some strings and I went to Jenks.

By the time Julia joined me in attending Jenks as a six-year-old, I was 12 and an old hand at public bus riding.

Oh, I'd had some mishaps with bus tickets, issued in strips of 10 in those days, one of which disintegrated into mushy pulp in my mittened hand during a long wait for a bus in a raging snowstorm when we'd been let out of school early. And, over the years, an occasional ticket had been lost, requiring a call home from a store begging for a pickup, but all in all I was a savvy user of public transportation.

When Julia started taking the bus with me, she became my responsibility. Every school morning, we walked one block to Stenton Avenue to catch the bus for the ride to Jenks. For the trip home, we had a prearranged meeting place in the schoolyard. We then walked the several blocks to the bus stop, boarded, and rode home. We usually sat together on the rides in both directions, but on one occasion when we were homeward bound and the bus was very crowded, we had to sit quite a distance apart. When the bus neared Vernon Road, I signaled the driver and got off. The bus departed and I looked behind me for Julia. She had not exited the bus! By the time I realized what had happened, the bus was already halfway into the next block. I strained my eyes to see if it stopped at Dorset Street. I would then walk down there to meet her. But the bus steamed right past the next stop.

For a moment, I was frozen with fear. Then, wild-eyed and on wobbly legs, I ran the one block home. I saw that my mother's car was not in the garage, so I did what I had never done before: I knocked on the closed door to the treatment room in Daddy's medical office. Although he was in the midst of treating a patient, he immediately came out and, seeing my stricken face, asked what was wrong. I blurted out in a rush of words and sobs that Julia hadn't gotten off the bus with me. My father excused himself from the patient, lying draped in a gown on the treatment table, and propelled me by the shoulder into the private part of our home.

"Tell me exactly what happened," he snapped.

"It was very crowded on the bus, and we weren't sitting together, and I thought she knew it was time to get off, but she didn't get off with me!" I gulped and sobbed some more. "I waited to see if she would get off at the next stop, but she didn't."

Daddy thought for a few minutes, then called the police to describe the situation. It took a really long time, and the police said they'd try to intercept the bus and take Julia off and bring her home. They asked if I knew the number of the bus, but of course I didn't. They would not have any way of knowing which bus Julia was on. And by now she was terribly far from home. My biggest fear was that she would get off the bus at some unknown point along the route and be wandering around lost or prey to

God only knows what. There was no end to the horrors I conjured.

I don't remember being resentful of having to accompany my younger sister on the bus every day. I wasn't a kid who disdained her younger siblings in front of others my age. I was a responsible—even ultra-responsible—child. There is no way that I would have done this deliberately. I was not angry at Julia for anything that day. I guess I assumed that after so many months of riding, she knew where to get off without my telling her. Maybe I was daydreaming and totally forgot Julia was even on the bus with me, since we weren't seated together. I've never figured out what led me to leave her on the bus that day.

Then my father had the idea to get in the car and follow the bus route, looking for Julia along the way. After a quick explanation to the patient, he commanded me to come with him, and we ran out of the house and to the garage. He backed his car out the driveway far too fast and we started up Vernon Road toward Stenton Avenue. As we neared that intersection, we saw an old woman and Julia walking toward our house. Julia was crying and the woman was holding her hand and talking to her. My father pulled the car over and jumped out, scooping Julia into his arms. He talked briefly with the woman, who explained that Julia had started crying on the bus and, when asked why, had told her that her sister had gotten off and left her behind. Luckily, my sister had been drilled in our street address, and the woman and Julia had gotten off the bus and walked many blocks back to our house. Daddy offered to drive the woman home, but she refused, so he gave her some bills for her return fare and thanked her profusely. He carried Julia back to the car, and then his relief at finding her gave way to his fury at me for losing her.

"What in the world were you thinking? We have put your sister into your care. You are responsible for her on that bus ride. Don't ever, ever again sit away from her on the bus, and don't ever, ever again get off the bus without making sure first that she's right with you." I just nodded my assent dumbly.

There was really no need for the lecture. I knew for certain that this was one experience that would never be repeated.

2004

Daddy Was Always Watching

My father's osteopathic practice—and its presence in our home—had an enormous impact on my life and that of my family. Except for the several mornings a week when he made house calls, taught a course to nurses at the college, or went to the hospital or a nursing home to visit a patient, Daddy was home all day every day and very much minding our business.

The treatment room had a frosted window that opened onto our driveway, a place where the raucous and noisy play of us three girls and our friends overflowed from our backyard. In warmer weather, my father opened that window for ventilation and could see us playing and with whom we were playing. Even if we were out of sight, he could identify our friends' voices—often at dinner, he commented on the bad language used outside that window

39

by so-and-so, or the angry words exchanged between X and Y. If things really got out of hand, he shouted out the window to shush us or chase us away.

When I was late coming home from a friend's, I was unable to sneak in the back door unobtrusively, as he always saw me walking up the driveway. If his hands were busy, as they usually were, he'd at least nod—and invariably check his watch. At dinner that night, I got a lecture or a punishment for my lateness.

Finally, unable to stand our commotion anymore, and bowing to the complaints of patients who said he dripped sweat on them while administering osteopathic manipulative treatment, he bought an air conditioner for the treatment room window and ended one phase of his intimate involvement in our lives.

Those were also the days when doors could be left open—and were. Perhaps it was less a case of the relative safety of the times and our neighborhood than the fact that a man was almost always present in the house—and all-seeing. A farmer, Mr. Moyer, a mountain of a man, delivered bacon, sausage, butter, eggs, and poultry every Friday. He came in our unlocked back door, read the list my mother left for him, put those items into our refrigerator, and left his bill. He would then pocket the money she left for him for the previous week's purchases. When we came home from school, we came in that same unlocked back door. And on those rare occasions when it was locked, we walked back around to the front and came in that way, since it was open for the patients.

When I was about 12, my father's secretary, Jannie, had to leave his employ because her only child was born with a severe birth defect, and Daddy did not replace her. Instead, he taught me to keep the books and paid me for doing so. After school and in the evenings, I did journal entries and added up columns and columns of figures in my head. Since I sat at his secretary's desk, I began to take on other aspects of her job. I greeted the patients when they came in, made out bills for them, receipted their paid bills, and made appointments. Actually, everyone in the family made appointments, even Julia and Gretchen when they became old enough.

We had only one phone line to serve both the medical practice and the family. We were restricted to five-minute personal phone calls because we couldn't tie up the line. Each of us knew how to answer the phone professionally, where the appointment book was kept, and how to schedule an appointment. We knew to ask the spelling of a name and for a telephone number. Actually, though, we rarely had to do that. Because the patients were almost all friends of the family's in addition to being my father's patients, their names were well known to us all. This was both good and bad.

Among Daddy's patients was a dear little old lady, Miss Henkels, who came once a week on the bus south from Chestnut Hill. She was a great baker and at every appointment brought us some home-baked treat. Her specialty was turning cupcakes upside down and icing everything but what had been the top, thus giving you a lot more icing than the normal way. We loved them!

She had the world's largest cat; it weighed in at around 25 pounds. Since we went to school in Chestnut Hill, sometimes we'd stop in to visit her, her cat, and her cookies. She had a house that was stereotypical for an "old maid" of that day—antimacassars on the chairs, darkening shades, overstuffed furniture in every available space, and piles of newspapers, magazines, and projects all over the house. And the house smelled of cat.

When she got too old to take the bus to my father, he went to her, and often took one of us along. By that time, her cat was also the world's oldest, and the devotion of those two souls to each other—old, old woman and old, old cat—was something to experience.

Some years later, when the devoutly Roman Catholic Miss Henkels was invited to my wedding—to be held in a Unitarian Universalist church—she went to her parish

My father, Anton Henry Claus.

priest to get permission to be there. She received it and attended.

Other wonderful characters came to receive my father's care. One, Mrs. Henry, was an older society matron, also from Chestnut Hill. She always complimented me profusely, embarrassing me, as I knew the things she said couldn't possibly be true. She was fabulously wealthy, Daddy told me. She drove an ancient station wagon with real wooden panels on the sides. She wore white or beige gloves at all times, even indoors, and wore something I've seen no one else wear before or since: a frowner. This was a square flesh-colored bandage in the middle of her forehead to keep her from frowning and getting forehead wrinkles.

The downside of the patients-as-friends model was that they seemed to be an extension of my father's watchfulness over us. I had a boyfriend with a motorcycle when I was studying at Temple University and living at home. My father did not permit me to ride on the motorcycle. But I would walk out of the house in the morning and go down a couple of blocks, and Bob would pick me up there—on the motorcycle. One of the patients—Daddy would never tell me who—saw me in traffic on Broad Street and told my father (maybe only *mentioned* it; perhaps "told" is too harsh a word).

Naturally, I was punished, and I have not been on a motorcycle since.

When Daddy decided in his 50s to give up his general practice to study psychiatry, his patients were beyond distraught. He was a charismatic man, a skilled and compassionate doctor, and he took the very best of care of each of his patients/friends. He always attended the occasional funeral, and when two patients died within days or weeks of each other, he would "wait for the other shoe to drop." He maintained that deaths came in threes.

By the time he saw his final patient in the treatment room in the office in our home, we three children were grown and no longer played in the driveway under that window.

Date unknown

The Unforgiven

My father worked as hard at play as he did at work, and he worked very, very hard. He was a general practitioner in the days when doctors still mostly worked alone rather than in group practices. In his office on the first floor of our family's home, he saw patients mornings, afternoons, and several evenings a week, and he reserved a half-day weekly for house calls. He saw only two patients an hour, giving each one an extended osteopathic treatment for the grand sum of $3.00 in the 1950s. After his secretary resigned, Daddy did much of the bookkeeping and other office work himself after hours, and trained me, his preteen firstborn, to assist with the paperwork. He also did all of the lawn and garden work around our large Mt. Airy home.

On one Wednesday, Daddy's day off, he was sweating profusely in shorts and a T-shirt in the front yard, propelling the push mower up and down the lawn in neat strips, when someone—his business now forgotten and of no importance—assuming my father to be the gardener, asked with what we would now call "attitude" for Dr. Claus. Daddy didn't suffer fools gladly and, quick to smell condescension, excused himself, went around to the back door, walked through the house, and opened the front door, still dripping. "I'm Dr. Claus," he said. "What can I do for you?"

My father wielded a mean paintbrush, and I, and later my much younger sisters, learned to handle a brush with equal skill at a fairly early age. We painted his waiting room and office every other year, and the rest of the house on a less stringent schedule. In the Poconos, we did all of the upkeep of our summer cottage, Dox, cleverly—at least we thought so—named in honor of the two doctors in the family. One summer, Daddy and I installed a post and rail fence between our backyard and the neighbor's, my father doing all of the post-hole digging by hand. He and my mother laid our large brick patio themselves, and I did much planting, weeding, and watering of plants. Friends and patients were amazed at the amount of work my father wrung from his children, and when they asked about it, were told, "They don't work, they don't eat." It was probably not that draconian a setup, but certainly none of us tested the premise.

One of Daddy's pleasures was music. He played the piano—as I did—and sang not only in his church choir but also with Singing City Choir, a multicultural, semiprofessional choir whose *raison d'être* was to break down racial and economic barriers through their music, both within the choir and in the community, where they regularly performed. Rehearsals were frequent and long. I often accompanied him, just to observe, listen, and learn.

So it was no surprise that when my father—always a lover of travel—discovered Mexico and the Spanish language, we all went along for the ride, especially me. Daddy taught himself Spanish with tapes and books, and in the days before faxes and email, actually made all of the family's Mexican travel plans himself, typing our family's requirements in Spanish on thin, crinkly onionskin paper, sending it off in a blue airmail envelope, then waiting patiently for a return letter.

The summer of my 18th year, the family was planning a two-week trip to Saltillo, Mexico, to board with a local family and to study Spanish at the university there. Excitement ran high and preparations went into overdrive. I started Spanish lessons with my father. He set up a classroom of sorts in a no-longer-used room on our third floor, across from my bedroom. I was given twice-weekly instruction, homework, and tests. I was an apt pupil, learning the language with little problem. Also, there was really no other option. While I doubt I would have been denied sustenance had I not conjugated the assigned verbs correctly, there was little tolerance for a less-than-stellar performance. I responded well to Daddy's accustomed pressure and perfectionism, and probably to the one-on-one time he lavished on me.

The verb "to be" has two forms in Spanish, *ser* to denote an essential characteristic—The chair is black (*La silla es negra*)—and *estar* to express a condition subject to change—I am sick today (*Estoy enferma hoy*). Learning under which circumstances to use these two irregular verbs, the bedrock of the language, not to mention learning their conjugations in all of the tenses, tested my mettle.

"The boy was busy."

El muchacho estuvo ocupado.

"He was also late."

El estaba también tarde.

"The girl was beautiful."

La muchacha era hermosa.

"It is nine o'clock in the morning."

Son las nueve de la mañana.

"It is exactly six o'clock."

Son las seis en punto.

The questions came faster; the pressure was on. I made frequent errors and was corrected. Finally, after using the wrong "to be" verb just one too many times, and being corrected just once too often, I screamed at my teacher— my father—"I can't do this anymore! I don't want to do this anymore! This is too difficult! I'm tired!" I accompanied this outburst with the unthinkable—I threw my pencil, not really at him, but in his direction. It struck him.

There was utter silence for a long, long time. I started to cry as my anger was replaced by guilt and fear. My father said not a word, but gathered up the Spanish books, tapes, blackboard, chalk, papers, and pens, and went downstairs.

The next day, after tearfully telling Mother of my transgression, I apologized to Daddy for throwing the pencil. But never was another syllable uttered in Spanish in that third-floor classroom.

2004

Ducks

One Easter, my sisters and I received six ducklings as a gift. My father rigged up a large chicken wire pen for them with a plastic wading pool in our backyard. I think the idea of the ducks was to train us in the care and feeding of animals, to teach us responsibility.

Several weeks later, my parents were away from Philadelphia for the weekend and our Auntie Jane, an older relative, was caring for us. On Saturday night, a terrible storm hit the area with thunder, lightning, and driving rain. Braving the storm, Auntie Jane went into the yard to put the ducks, two at a time, into a box and bring them into the house. She turned on the oven to its very lowest setting, dried the ducks with towels as best she could, and put them into the oven with the door open to dry and warm them. Unfortunately, three of the ducks died. Auntie Jane was very upset when my parents returned, as she felt responsible.

Because the remaining ducks always walked around the yard in single file, we named them Quacky, Wacky, and Stay-Behind.

Some time later, one of us left the gate open and the ducks escaped. Before their disappearance was noticed, they had walked over a mile, single file, up our very busy street. One of Daddy's patients saw them and called, and we all jumped into the car to round them up. In the meantime, someone had called the weekly *Germantown Courier*, and a few days later, the newspaper ran a photo of our ducks and a story about their escape and long walk.

Julia and I with the ducks in our backyard in Philadelphia. This photo appeared in the local weekly newspaper, The Germantown Courier, after the ducks escaped, walked over a mile, and were rounded up.

Analomink Lake, in the Pennsylvania Pocono Mountains, where we had
a summer cottage, bought the same year that Gretchen was born, 1952.

Our cottage, Dox, on Analomink Lake, named for the owners, my parents, two doctors.
At some point in this photo's history, it must have been printed backward,
as DOX now says XOD.

When summer came, Gretchen, Julia, Mother, and the ducks went up to our cabin in the Poconos. They stayed there all summer, whereas Daddy and I were working during the week and commuted up and back for the weekends. The ducks loved the lake. They swam, they flew, and they honked, but they always returned home for breakfast and dinner. My mother would go down to the dock and make some sort of call that they responded to. And then they'd waddle up from the lake to our cottage one after the other, and we'd feed them. They had total freedom, and over the summer they became full-grown.

Summer ended, and as we were packing up to return to the city, Daddy, unbeknownst to us, took the ducks to be butchered. He then took them to Philadelphia and put them in our freezer. When we inquired about the ducks, he told us that they could not possibly survive a harsh mountain winter nor could we keep them anymore in Philadelphia, and that he had had them butchered. We were upset but it all seemed to make sense at the time, and we would not have questioned our father's decision anyway. With the chaos of moving back to Philadelphia, we let our memories of the ducks rest. But we certainly never dreamed that they were in our freezer.

One Sunday evening in the fall, we had dinner as a family as usual. What was unusual was that Daddy

*Daddy feeding our ducks, Quacky, Wacky, and Stay-Behind,
at Dox. Notice the smoke from my father's
ever-present cigarette.*

cooked—a duck. When he brought it to the table with great flourish, he announced that it was one of our ducks and began to carve it. We were horrified! We all cried and screamed and carried on. None of us would touch the duck meat except my father, who seemed to relish it and told us how good it was. I don't know what happened to the two other frozen ducks, but we didn't see them at our dinner table.

In thinking about this story years later, I believe that the cruel part was not the butchering; the offering of our pet to us as a meal was the cruel part. Our father could have given or sold them to the butcher and not brought them home. Obviously he viewed them as livestock while we three sisters and our mother viewed them as beloved pets. We had given them names. They were famous, for heaven's sake; their picture had been in the paper and the topic of conversation in the neighborhood for weeks. If my father had told us from the beginning that they were to be butchered at the end, it might have been different.

Oddly, I can't remember who gave us the ducklings in the first place, and that is probably a vital part of the story. Was it Daddy? He often disparaged people who gave chicks and ducks and such as pets for Easter, which led to families having to abandon them to the SPCA as the animals matured and grew less fuzzy and lovable, not to mention children's promises to take care of them fading into boredom and neglect. And yet, who else would have saddled a family with six ducks?

I wonder now if he did tell us in the beginning of his plan to raise them to maturity and then butcher them. Perhaps we didn't believe that he would do that or we just put it out of our minds. I want to believe that he did tell us; otherwise, what he did is just too cruel to bear.

My parents, Anton and Eleanor Claus, in their work clothes at Dox.

And where was my mother in all of this? Was the plan to butcher and eat the ducks not discussed with her, just as it was not discussed with us three children? Did she try to talk my father out of it, point out to him how hurtful it would be to us girls? If she knew, why didn't she tell us the truth? Or was she as afraid of my father as we three daughters were? We will never know.

Date unknown

Life with Daddy

I know next to nothing about my father's life as a boy or how he came up with the unusual and often repressive rules and schemes he employed to keep his three daughters toeing the line. I adhered to some of these and developed coping mechanisms and work-arounds for the others. I offer a few examples. You can judge for yourself.

If we left anything lying around our house, Daddy picked it up and kept it somewhere until the following Saturday, when we had the weekly buy-back session. He took out the articles of clothing, toys, books, whatever, one by one from a bag, and set prices that we had to pay to get them back. If you needed one of those things before Saturday, that was your tough luck.

We had to eat everything on our plates. I frequently put things like liver or cauliflower into my napkin and then excused myself to go to the bathroom to flush the food down the toilet. Or, sometimes, I could slip it to the dog. Once, at a dinner party my parents gave for good friends, and to which I was invited as the oldest child by several years, scallops were served. It was my first experience with scallops, and I absolutely shivered at the taste of them, so awful did they seem to me. I kind of pushed them around on my plate, and ate everything else, and thought that maybe in front of company, I was going to get away scot-free leaving them on my plate, but as the dishes were being cleared, Daddy, who had had quite a bit to drink by that time, asked me why my scallops remained uneaten. I told him that I had tried them but that I didn't like the taste of them, and I just couldn't eat them.

In front of the company, he insisted that I eat them. The tension around the table was palpable. Everyone else's plates were taken away and dessert was brought in. Still the uneaten scallops sat on the plate in front of me. There was to be no dessert for me until I had eaten the scallops. Mother tried to intervene, but my father insisted that she stay out of it and that I had to clean my plate. I took another tiny bite, gagged, and had to spit it out. I just couldn't eat it. The situation became more and more uncomfortable for everyone. Our guests left for home immediately after dinner as my father had spoiled what had been a lovely evening. I sat in my chair with the scallops in front of me for hours after they left. I could not eat them under any circumstances. Finally, Daddy told me to get up and go to bed.

For decades afterward, I could not stand the sight or the smell or even the thought of scallops. And then, in my 60s, I was served them at a friend's house and they smelled and looked good. I decided to try to get beyond my deeply entrenched loathing. I served myself just one, cut off the smallest piece I possibly could, and tentatively put it in my mouth. It was sweet, tender, and delicious! I almost cried for joy. I took and enjoyed more scallops, and felt as if I had exorcised forever the horrible memory of that dreadful dinner party.

In Daddy's world, movies and sunshine didn't mix. On sunny days, my sisters and I were not allowed to go to the movies; we had to be outside playing. In inclement weather, there was no problem. Even now, when I go to the movies on a sunny afternoon, I feel guilty and somewhat risqué.

We three daughters and our mother spent the summers in the Poconos in the first years that we owned Dox, while my father worked in Philadelphia and came for Wednesday, his day off, and the weekends. Daddy loved to fish, and we had a lovely big old wooden rowboat that came with the place, which he took out very early on Saturdays and Sundays for hours, just enjoying the dawn and the peace and quiet, casting his rod repeatedly in the hope of catching some bass or perch for breakfast. The rest of the family slept in. When he returned, he came into our rooms and held the fish he caught—usually an ugly, gaping large-mouthed bass—inches from our sleeping faces and then shook us awake. There was nothing quite as frightening as awakening to that sight so close to my nearsighted eyes, and I never failed to scream, which was undoubtedly the desired result.

None of us was ever allowed not to be busy; we always had to be doing something constructive. At Dox, our next-door neighbor Cliff frequently sat in his yard in an Adirondack chair for hours on the weekends, doing absolutely nothing. My father was horrified! "Look at Cliff," he'd say derisively, pointing his way. "He is just sitting there. He's not even reading!" I learned that lesson well! To this day, it is very hard for me to relax, and I feel a little panicky if I don't have a full roster of activities each and every day. And yes, to this day, I judge people who, for example, sit idly, doing nothing but watching the scenery pass by on an eight-hour train ride, while I, of course, read.

One day when I was about 12, Daddy announced that we would be reading *Time* magazine together weekly. We started with just the cover article. I was to read it, look up any words I didn't know the meaning of, and be prepared to take a test on content and vocabulary. That went on for several months, and then I was to read the cover article and another of my choosing. The tests on content and vocabulary continued. Finally, it was the cover article and two other articles of my choice. We kept up this routine for several years, until it eventually petered out when I had too many activities and too much homework to allow any time for *Time* magazine.

Because my father's medical practice was in our home, and because after a certain point, he did not have a secretary, he installed a buzzer on the front door so that he would know, from inside the treatment room, when the next patient arrived. We also had a grandfather's clock in the waiting room, which gonged every 15 minutes in an ever-increasing length, until at the top of the hour the entire Westminster Chimes played. I used this buzzer and gong combination to my advantage when I came in from a date, hoping not to waken my father and have to talk about where I had gone with my boyfriend. We stood outside the door and listened for the chime of the clock. I then opened the door, and the sound of the buzzer was disguised in the notes of the clock's chimes. Luckily, since I was generally returning at 10 or 11 o'clock, I had more than enough time to get in with the many chimes counting out the hour. In this manner, if my parents were already asleep, I could enter the house without waking them, as they were quite used to sleeping through the chimes.

Daddy insisted on truthfulness at all times and in all situations. He stressed that if I told the truth, there would be no repercussions. One night, I got in 15 minutes late from a date. I did the chimes-covering-the-buzzer routine and got up to my room unscathed. The next morning, my father asked me what time I got in. Having learned that truthfulness was always the way to go, I told him that I was 15 minutes late, and I was punished for that infraction.

During my freshman year at Gettysburg College, Daddy wrote me long, deeply detailed letters every week. I needed a dictionary to look up many of the words contained in them, and they were so different from the usual letters from a father that I read them out loud to my three roommates, who howled with laughter. I think my father's purpose in this was to show how intellectual he was and how he wanted to share that intellectual vibrancy with me;

how much he loved me and missed me; and how high his expectations were for me. This practice perpetuated the appearance of a loving, caring, nurturing father, without the downside of alcoholism, mental illness, and strangling control.

When Suresh and I were newly married, I became extremely sick with a fierce sinus infection, and I made an appointment with my father. Suresh drove me there and stayed in the waiting room to drive me home. It was the first time Daddy had seen me as a patient since I left home. When he came out of the treatment room with the previous patient, he looked at me very strangely and then said, "I didn't recognize you; you are so sick." He did what we in our family had always laughingly called "the horror treatment." He pushed strips of cotton saturated with some medication that shrinks the nasal passages up into my sinus cavities and left them there for the remainder of the treatment, necessitating mouth breathing. Then there was the osteopathic manual medicine, hands-on manipulation of the spine for 20 minutes or so to correct any neuroskeletal dysfunction to allow the body to heal itself naturally. He then removed the cotton, and I blew out copious mucus. He wrote me a prescription for antibiotics and told me to drink lots of fluids and to rest. I thanked him profusely and we went home.

Not a week later, I received a professional envelope from him in the mail. I was curious to see what was in it. Was I ever surprised when a bill for his services fell out. I was angry and disillusioned and spent lots of time screaming in fury at poor Suresh, who said that of course we would immediately pay it, which we did. Very soon after that, I signed on with another osteopath in the neighborhood and never visited Daddy again as my doctor.

It was one of many endings in my life with my father.

Date unknown

ICE CREAM & PRETZELS

REGRET I
How Could Anyone Know?

Looking at their wedding pictures now, it is hard to imagine their marriage as I experienced it. In the black-and-white photos, he is handsome in a dark suit, tie, and white boutonniere, his rimless glasses reflecting the light of the flash. He has a thin mustache that I never saw—and don't much like the looks of now—and wonderful dark hair. She looks very much like me, or rather I look very much like her. She is wearing a simple white silk gown, a veil clipped to the back of her rolled hair, and pearls. She looks adoringly at him. She has beautiful teeth, but her eyebrows look artificially dark, '40s-style. They are my parents.

They were married in my grandmother's living room in March 1942, probably when my father was home on leave. Perhaps because it was wartime, it was a very small wedding; each parent had only one attendant. Oddly, the engraved card that my grandmother sent out afterward announced that her daughter, Eleanor Elizabeth, was married to Dr. Anton H. Claus. Why was my mother not listed as a doctor, also? In a newspaper clipping describing the event, however, the headline reads "Two Doctors Wed Saturday," and the first line begins "Dr. Eleanor E. Boal…"

In their wedding photos, they are both in their late twenties, both doctors, and both an only child, but the similarities end there. My father was raised by second-generation Germans. Although English was the language of the house, lots of German expressions were still liberally used. Daddy's name was the epitome of Germanness— Anton Henry Claus. My father's grandfather on his mother's side had been an officer in the Prussian army, and I believe Daddy's upbringing reflected a certain German precision and discipline. My father's father, Henry John

67

Mrs. William Boal

announces the marriage of her daughter

Eleanor Elizabeth

to

Doctor Anton H. Claus

on Saturday, the fourteenth of March

nineteen hundred and forty-two

Philadelphia, Pennsylvania

My parents' wedding announcement.
This was sent out in lieu of a big wedding,
as it was during wartime.

ENGAGED

Mrs. William Boal, of Mt. Airy, announces the engagement of her daughter, Dr. Eleanor Elizabeth Boal, to Dr. Anton H. Claus, son of Mr. and Mrs. Henry J. Claus, of Oak Lane. Dr. Boal is a graduate of the Philadelphia College of Osteopathy. Dr. Claus, who attended the University of Pennsylvania and Temple University, is also a graduate of the Philadelphia College of Osteopathy.

Announcement of my parents' engagement,
probably in The Philadelphia Inquirer.

Two Doctors Wed Saturday

Daughter of Mrs. William Boal United in Marriage to Dr. Anton Claus in Home Ceremony

Dr. Eleanor E. Boal, daughter of Mrs. William Boal, 518 E. Durham St., was married Saturday afternoon to Dr. Anton H. Claus of the Osteopathic Hospital, son of Mr. and Mrs. Henry Claus, 6816 N. 10th St. The ceremony was performed at the home of the bride's mother by the Rev. Max Bascom of the Unitarian Church on Lincoln Drive.

The bride was gowned in broaded ivory satin, made on princess lines. The bodice was trimmed with pearls and had long sleeves. The full skirt ended in a short train. Real gardenias held the fingertip veil to her hair. She carried white flowers.

Miss Blanche Fiechter was maid of honor. She was gowned in turquoise blue taffeta and had American beauty colored accessories and carried blending flowers.

Mr. Wallace Weingartned was best man for Dr. Claus. There were no ushers.

Mrs. Boal chose a violet sheer gown and wore a corsage of orchids. The bridegroom's mother wore a pale gray gown and an orchid corsage.

There was a reception for the family following the ceremony.

Announcement of my parents' marriage,
probably in The Philadelphia Inquirer.

Mother on her wedding day, March 14, 1942.

Mother and Daddy on their wedding day, March 14, 1942.

Claus, was a kind, sweet, loving man who owned a florist shop with his brother, John, and their mother, until she died. She was somewhat of a tyrant, I was given to understand. Maybe that was why my grandfather married another one, my Grossmama, Marie Antoinette Euhr. Pop Pop called her "Toots." She ruled the roost in her home. Grossmama had a spectacular figure well into her 70s, and dressed impeccably to accentuate it. She had perfect posture and was always well-groomed and coiffed. She kept an immaculate and beautifully furnished home and cooked wonderful meals, but was not what you'd describe as "warm." But she certainly loved me and my two sisters.

My grandfather, on the other hand, often looked rumpled and bent over. He had extraordinary thick, white hair. His hands and fingernails were permanently blackened from spending so much time in soil. Whenever he came to our house, Mother took his dirt-speckled glasses from him and gave them a good washing. When my sisters and I were little, my mother took us to the flower shop near major holidays—Christmas and Easter. Pop Pop was extremely busy, but he took the time to make a fuss over us, to introduce us around to the employees and any customers, and then to lead us through the greenhouse with its smells of dampness, warmth, and soil. And always when we left, each of us was clutching

My paternal grandparents, Henry John
Claus (Pop Pop) and Marie Euhr Claus
(Grossmama), vacationing in Florida.

Grossmama

Greenhouse at Claus Bros. Florists in North Philadelphia, 1957.

71

a miniature clay pot containing a tiny plant. It was only very much later that I learned that he was an alcoholic. An old family friend told me, years after Pop Pop's death. He was surprised that I didn't know.

My mother, Eleanor Boal, was raised by a warm, extremely overweight mother and an English father. William Boal—16 years older than his wife, Florence Bell Boal—died at the age of 57 and was buried on my mother's 17th birthday. His life is a totally blank slate to me. He came from England and had a grocery or bakery business of some sort that is thought to have morphed into the American Baking Company, and finally into Acme, the grocery store chain, but no proof exists of this. I don't remember Gramma or Mother ever saying anything about him to me at all except for one vivid story. In it, he was explaining the method and delights of eating corn on the cob: "First, you roll up your sleeves, then you slather the hot corn with butter and add lots of salt. Lean way out over the table so as to let the juices fall onto your plate." I envision a somewhat buttoned-up Englishman, wearing a long-sleeved shirt in the middle of summer— corn season—and, with a twinkle in his eye, giving this guidance to visiting relatives from England who may not ever have eaten corn on the cob before.

I have a total of four photos of him. In three, he is in a

My mother and her father,
William Boal.

My maternal grandfather,
William Boal.

suit with the jacket buttoned. Only one picture shows him in shirtsleeves, and they are long. It appears to be spring or summer and he's standing with a black Scottie dog in the backyard of his home. In one of these four photos he's with my mother, probably in her early teens; she's quite chubby. In another he's with his wife, my grandmother; she's excessively stout, as she always was as long as I knew her. He is handsome, showing only the barest suggestion of a smile, and is not touching either of the women in his life or the dog.

My most vivid memory of Gramma was her sitting in an upholstered chair in her living room, reading a hardback book with a Whitman's Chocolate Sampler open next to her, from which she indulged repeatedly. She was the opposite of Grossmama in looks and demeanor. Because she was obese, she had to have her dresses custom-made. A dressmaker would come periodically with samples of materials, and a long measuring session would follow. The fabrics were exquisite in color and texture, and the dresses were draped skillfully, but there was no hiding Gramma's girth. She was sentimental and cried at the drop of a hat. I remember well her tears on those Christmases when she tore the paper off her present of a professionally posed photo of us three girls, frequently wearing identical dresses. I never understood those tears until I had my own

My maternal grandparents,
Florence and William Boal.

Gramma

Mother

grandchildren and did exactly the same thing!

Photos of my mother at the time her father died show her in a thick fur-collared coat standing next to a roadster that was hers. She was raised in some wealth and became accustomed to elegance and gentility. She had elocution lessons. When my sisters and I were girls, we would beg her to recite the difficult "Jabberwocky" by Lewis Carroll:

'Twas brillig, and the slithy toves
Did gyre and gimble in the wabe:
All mimsy were the borogoves,
And the mome raths outgrabe.

"Beware the Jabberwock, my son!
The jaws that bite, the claws that catch!
Beware the Jubjub bird, and shun
The frumious Bandersnatch!"...

Although my parents were only four months apart in age, lived in the same neighborhood as children, and went to the same elementary school, they didn't know each other then. Actually, I don't know how they met. But friends told me they were gaga for each other, so in love were they. I also learned that even then they drank a lot.

Daddy was drafted into the Naval Reserves immediately upon his 1941 graduation from the Philadelphia College of Osteopathy, and worked in tropical disease control in New Guinea, Australia, and Trinidad. He must also have been in the Philippines, as I remember him showing me Filipino money that he saved from that time. My father told this story resentfully: that in 1941, during the war, the Navy did not recognize his doctorate in osteopathic medicine and surgery, and so he did not enter the Navy as a doctor but rather as a medic or corpsman. He did not talk much about his years in the service. He refused to eat creamed chipped beef—he'd eaten enough in the Navy to last a lifetime—and he wouldn't attend displays of Independence Day fireworks with the rest of the family, as it reminded him too much of what he'd experienced during the war.

I came along in August 1943, about a year and a half after their marriage. Mother put her medical practice on hold and we went to live in San Diego near Daddy's base until he shipped out to the South Pacific. Mother and I then returned to Philadelphia to live with my widowed grandmother and her unmarried sister, Aunt Ethel. I do not remember anything of Auntie Ethel except her very thick ankles, probably because I was crawling around near them much of the time. For years, I was fawned over by these three adoring females. Meanwhile, my mother made a name for herself as a

Mother with me, age 6 months.

*Three generations: Gramma, Mother,
and I in Gramma's backyard in
East Mt. Airy, Philadelphia, when I was
9 months old.*

*Mother and I at a New Jersey beach when
I was 11 months old.*

Mother and I, age 9 months, on the side of Gramma's home.

Mother and I.

general practitioner with a special flair for pediatrics.

Daddy was present for my birth and earliest days, as there are pictures of him holding me at one day old, at seven weeks and again at 10 weeks, but then not again until I was 17 months old. Those last photos were taken in San Diego; my father is in his naval uniform.

A story I heard from my father many times over the years was that on August 14, 1945, he told his buddies that the war was going to end that day, as it was his daughter's birthday, and darned if it didn't! Victory over Japan (VJ Day) was declared on the day I turned two, just a few days after the U.S. dropped the atom bomb on Hiroshima and Nagasaki. The next time my photo album shows a picture of me with my father, it is June 1946, when I was nearly three years old.

When Daddy returned from the war, my parents bought

Daddy and I, age 17 months, in San Diego, California, where my father was stationed during World War II.

a large twin house of Wissahickon schist on Vernon Road, just blocks from where Mother and I had been living with Gramma. The front portion of the house was remodeled to accommodate my parents' joint general medical practice, and my mother gave up her office in Chestnut Hill. But my father was already bitter at having his career path interrupted by nonmedical service in the Navy for so many years while my mother's practice had taken off, and the joint practice never really worked. His monumental ego crushed hers and she couldn't keep up.

After the difficult delivery of their second daughter, Julia, in 1949, Mother had what was then termed a nervous breakdown—probably postpartum depression—was hospitalized, and received shock therapy. She never resumed her medical career. She hung her medical diploma in the basement over the washing machine. At each successive house in which they lived, she displayed it in the same place. An older maiden lady, Aunt Gertie, was installed on our third floor in a small apartment to provide childcare and other needed services. These two "inadequacies" painted my mother as a failure, both at being a doctor and being a mother.

Mother didn't do a lot of things the mothers of my friends did; she wasn't much of a mother in the traditional sense. She felt she was so much older than the other mothers of elementary school-aged kids that she refused to participate in things like the PTA. She definitely wasn't a cookie baker or a stay-at-home mom. Aunt Gertie stayed on for years after the 1952 birth of my youngest sister, Gretchen, giving my mother a great deal of freedom. She—who had been so bright that she was permitted to go directly from high school to medical school with only advanced science courses in the summer between, and

731 Vernon Road, East Mt. Airy, Philadelphia, the house where Daddy had his medical practice and where we three daughters grew up.

My parents and I in front of our home on Vernon Road.

who had been so ahead of her time, one of only a handful of women in her class at medical school—became a woman who played. She joined the bowling-in-the-winter, golf-in-the-summer crowd, and played bridge and attended fashion show/luncheon parties year-round, although she was not fashionable. Clearly, being a mother was not her first choice. What was so infuriating about this for me was that that wasn't who my mother really was. Without her medical practice to sustain her, her life became vapid and meaningless. What she was was a devastating role model for us three daughters. I am guessing that during this period she stopped any pretense of fighting alcohol's power over her.

Life in our home, while it certainly had its good points, was difficult. My parents fought fiercely, much of the time about money, but also there clearly were differences in child-rearing strategies. When I was eight or nine, Daddy bought me an alarm clock, taught me how to use it, and put me in charge of getting him up in the morning. When the alarm went off on school mornings, I would go downstairs to waken him. I had to listen carefully when I went back upstairs to make sure that he did actually get up. To this day, I have "getting-up anxiety" when I have to rise at a very early hour to catch a plane, for example. I cannot sleep at all. I once had a therapist who was so angry when I told her the alarm clock story that I thought she was going to choke.

I was witness to violence between them. They seemed locked in some rancorous struggle and in their hate for each other. What bound them together was alcohol. They both drank excessively but reacted differently to it. When all of us girls were in school and Aunt Gertie no longer with us, Mother was unable to rise in the morning to get us off for the day. I, as the eldest, was pressed into service along with Daddy to serve breakfast and pack lunches. More than once, I had to pick my mother up off the floor and ease her into bed when she passed out, drunk. I told her before my wedding day that if she appeared at the service drunk, I would leave. She was sober. Daddy, on the other hand, drank at night until he was bleary-eyed and incoherent, but would be up every morning, back to his usual self and ready to work a full day. I became very adept at "reading" him, judging, when I came in from a date, how much he'd had to drink and how I should play our encounter.

One by one, we three girls escaped this vision of hell, my youngest sister, Gretchen, marrying at 18. In late middle age, Daddy decided to give up his general practice of 25 years and go back to school to become a psychiatrist. He said that he figured about 85 percent of his practice was psychiatric anyway; he might as well be doing it right. I've often wished he could have healed himself. He moved with Mother to West Chester, Pennsylvania, to intern at Embreeville State Hospital, a psychiatric facility. While he was busy and fulfilled, my mother had lost her friends, activities, and support system. Visits were painful for me, even with the grandchildren in tow. It was so obvious how far apart my parents were, how much they loathed being together. They said terribly hurtful things to each other.

The other thing they had in common was smoking, which they gave up together after 40 years of two packs a day each. It was too late by then for my mother, who died of metastasized lung cancer at age 64. Daddy's Alzheimer's disease became apparent immediately after my mother's death, when she was no longer running interference for him. His employment as a psychiatrist at Philhaven in Lebanon County, Pennsylvania, had to be terminated on the seventh anniversary of his hiring. Then, after a long, slow decline from the disease over another seven years, he died at age 71.

I look again at the wedding photos, searching for their future in their faces. I do not see it. Can we ever see it when love is new, before the years take their toll? Would we even want to?

2004

My Mothers

One day, while sitting wet-headed and toweled, I told my hairdresser, of all people, that because of alcoholism and dysfunction my mother had not been available to me much of the time I was growing up. He stopped cutting my hair and came around from behind to look me full in the face. "Don't you know, Cynthia," he said, "that there will be many mothers for you in your life?"

Now this particular hairdresser tended to be mightily new age, and much of what he said, I couldn't follow. I even took my business elsewhere because of this. But that one sentence, uttered when I was in my 40s, has haunted me, and I've come recently to appreciate the truth of it.

I *have* had many mothers in my life, although all are now dead. In my early years there were Aunt Gertie and Jannie Henninger, then more recently, Gisha Berkowitz and Helen Smith. Lillian Kushmore and Molly Baush Hill were part of my life for many decades. Of course, there was also my mother's own mother, Gramma.

Aunt Gertie came into my life soon after my first sister, Julia, was born when I was six years old. My mother had postpartum psychosis soon after the birth and was in a hospital where she was administered shock treatment. I don't know where Aunt Gertie came from, or how she got to us, but the arrangement was the answer to a prayer for all of us. She had little money and needed a place to live. We needed a caretaker for an infant and a first-grader. Aunt Gertie—Gertrude Wallace was her real name—was short and plump, with white hair. She was, as we said then, an old maid, probably in her 70s. Her apartment, on the third floor of our home, consisted of a bedroom and a combination kitchen/sitting room. She and I shared the bathroom, as my bedroom was right across the hall from her rooms. Since I was now the older sister and would have the comfort of a nearby presence, I was moved up there when Aunt Gertie came to live with us.

Probably because of years of necessity, Aunt Gertie knew how to pinch every penny until it squealed. She made candy out of grapefruit rind. I can see and taste it to this day—bitter, biting, crunchy, sugary, weird, and delicious. She was an accomplished seamstress and taught me how

Aunt Gertie and my youngest sister, Gretchen, age 1.

Lillian Kushmore

to thread a needle, despite my as-yet-undiagnosed severe nearsightedness and astigmatism. We cut and sewed doll clothes. We baked. But the best part, the part I remember with complete clarity, was how she took care of me when I was sick.

Being the child of two physicians made me a classic case of the cobbler's child with no shoes. Sickness in family members was not acknowledged in my house. You had to be on your deathbed to be allowed to miss school. Not even an extremely high fever excused you from piano practice. I had perfect attendance in junior high school in spite of crippling menstrual cramps every single month. Meals were never served to you in bed, regardless of your condition. You received nothing approaching TLC. With Aunt Gertie, all was different. She fluffed my pillow, washed my fevered face with a cool cloth, sat on the edge of my bed and talked to me, and brought me magazines from her homey collection, but best of all, she made me tea and served it in a clear glass cup and saucer. She sweetened it with sugar and added a few drops of lemon, then sat with me while I drank it. Few sights can inspire in me a feeling of warmth, caring, and contentment quicker than the sight of a hot amber liquid in a clear glass cup.

Three years later, another sister, Gretchen, arrived. Aunt Gertie was now a fixture at our house. My father teased her unmercifully. Those were the days when perked coffee was in vogue. There is a thin line between perking coffee and boiling it, and Aunt Gertie regularly allowed the coffee to cross that line. Daddy would bellow, "Gertrude, you're boiling the damn coffee again!" and Aunt Gertie would bustle over to the stove to adjust the flame. She always bustled in the kitchen. She could not work without making a lot of racket, particularly rattling and banging pots and pans. This also drove my father crazy, and he always let her know of his irritation with the din.

The years passed and Aunt Gertie got too old to be the caretaker; we were taking care of her. We moved her into the Presbyterian Home way out in West Philadelphia. We visited her fairly regularly at first, but then the visits dwindled off. I was a teenager by then, perhaps even off to college, and visiting old ladies was not high on my list of things to do. One day we got the call that she had died, and we attended her funeral. Aunt Gertie always said that Gretchen was her baby. That may have been, but for years, Aunt Gertie was my mother.

Janice Henninger—Jannie to my family—worked in our home as my father's secretary for his medical practice. She lived just in the next block, in an apartment. The apartment culture was intriguing to me, what with opening a little door in the wall with a tiny key to get your mail, riding the elevator up to your floor, and arriving in the somewhat-cheerless hallway to face down a forbidding row of identical closed doors from which emanated alien smells.

Jannie lived in the apartment with her husband, Lester. They did not have a baby for a long time, so she sort of adopted me. She often invited me to her apartment for dinner and the evening. We sat at her small kitchen table, where we looked down on our block from high above the trees. After dinner, we played cards or just talked while she ironed. I begged her to let me iron. She started me off with handkerchiefs and bureau scarves, and because I was such a willing and meticulous pupil, she let me go on to more intricate articles of clothing.

Jannie finally did have a baby, but the child had severe physical problems, and Jannie had to stop working for my father to take care of her full time. Daddy never replaced her. Instead, he did without a secretary during office hours and trained me to do the bookkeeping, billing, and banking, which I completed in the evenings and on weekends.

I met Jannie on the street once, years later. We each saw the other from afar and waved. When we got close, Jannie said something I've never forgotten. "I knew it was you, Cynthia, just by the way you walk, carefully putting one foot in front of the other, like you're walking a straight and narrow line." And, indeed, she was right. We all had to walk a straight and narrow line in my house, following seemingly arbitrary, vexing rules.

Over the years, even though they moved out of the immediate neighborhood, we kept in touch with Jannie and her family, particularly at Christmas. Daddy would take us three girls down to her house in Germantown and we'd visit for an hour or so, eating cookies and exchanging gifts. Even as an adult, I kept up the habit of sending her Christmas cards. Decades passed, but I never saw Jannie again.

Then, when my son was a young adult, he rented a room from a woman in Germantown, and when he told me the address, I shivered. It was directly across the street from Jannie's. I asked his landlady about the Henningers, and she told me that she had bought her house from them but that Jannie had just died. I wrote to Lester of the coincidence, and of my sorrow that Jannie had passed from my life just when it appeared that we were going to reconnect. He wrote back and gave me some details of her death. She had died of Alzheimer's disease, just as my father had. I wrote back to him that Jannie had been one of my mothers, that she had taught me how to iron and that I was a good ironer.

Lillian Kushmore, the mother of the maid of honor at my first wedding, Helen, was my friend until she died in her 90s, when I was 65. Some years earlier, Lillian moved to California to be closer to her son, Bob, and soon afterward, I sent her a Mother's Day card, the first I'd sent to anyone other than my own mother. It was one of those cards that say "You were like a mother to me." I wrote to her how much her mothering had meant as I was growing up and that her moving away had triggered in me a fresh realization of the hole in my life caused by the absence of my mother, which she had helped to fill.

For a couple of my teenage years, I practically lived at the Kushmores'. Helen was my best friend, and I had a crush on Bob—what a powerful combination that was. Theirs was not a perfect household, and I knew that, but the Kushmore home was the one in the neighborhood always filled with kids. The entire basement was turned over to us. We played records and danced down there. Food was readily available. And, unobtrusively, Lillian was *there*. I can remember spending hours in the kitchen talking to her. She baked a lot and kept the products in the freezer to pull out at a moment's notice when needed.

Lillian was another seamstress in my life. After I was married and we newlyweds moved into our apartment, she took me shopping for drapery material. She spent several days teaching me to make pinch-pleat drapes. We didn't use pleater tape; she actually taught me how to sew the pinch pleats into the curtains.

My mother's mother, Gramma, just plain adored me! There is no other way to say it. Of course, my mother and I lived with Gramma for some years while my father was in the service. When Daddy came home and we moved out, we visited her frequently, and she always had pennies "hidden" on the metal crumb catchers under the gas burners in her stove. I would run right to the kitchen and pull out those four drawers, which somehow miraculously never had any crumbs on them, and pocket the many pennies Gramma had put there for me. Also just for me was the bottom drawer of her Chippendale slant-front desk in the living room. I could push back the chair a little, slide in under the lowered writing surface, and open the drawer to find it full of toys, coloring books, and crayons, seemingly new and different things added to the old favorites every time. I could be happily absorbed for hours in that tiny cavelike space as the adults talked.

Another favorite of mine was her record player, which was, I think, formerly a wind-up player refitted with electricity. She had children's records for me, and allowed me to put them on the turntable and carefully lower the arm with the needle in it. She never complained when I played the same songs over and over. Her upright piano was also in the living room—oh, how I loved her piano! Starting at age six, I took some piano lessons and could read simple musical tunes, so of course there were books of musical selections for children waiting for me on the music stand. One that I played and that we sang together repeatedly was "Jesus Wants Me for a Sunbeam."

Jesus wants me for a sunbeam, a sunbeam, a sunbeam;
Jesus wants me for a sunbeam, to shine for him each day.
Jesus wants me for a sunbeam, a sunbeam, a sunbeam;
Jesus wants me for a sunbeam, at home, at school, at play.
Jesus wants me for a sunbeam, a sunbeam, a sunbeam;
Jesus wants me for a sunbeam; I'll be a sunbeam for him!

Gramma didn't drive, but she had a large, snazzy Buick in her garage. She disliked asking people to pick her up in their cars and take her somewhere, so she'd invite them over to drive her in her car, so she'd be paying for gas and upkeep, maintaining her dignity. Then she'd either provide lunch or take them out as a thank-you.

When I got older, I walked the few blocks to Gramma's house alone, and she and I played canasta. That's probably not a good card game to play with only two people, but we loved it. How I shrieked when I beat her!

When my parents bought our cabin in the Poconos,

Gramma rented a room at the posh Buck Hill Inn nearby for a month, and we often went to swim in the hotel's pool and have a lovely lunch with her. About a decade later, Gramma struggled with cancer for 18 months and died at age 78, eight months after the birth of my first child, Ajay. I have a couple of photos of her holding him, she in a much depleted state, but obviously thrilled with her first great-grandchild.

Two of my "mothers" recently died, both at very close to 90 years old. Gisha Berkowitz was my (nothing like a) boss when I worked at the Alternative East High School, a desegregation demonstration program of the Philadelphia School District and a clutch of suburban districts, located in a vacant elementary school just minutes over the city line in Wyndmoor. I started working with Gisha on my 35th birthday, in 1978. She was the head, and I was her assistant. For about three years, we spent an enormous amount of time together. We carpooled to and from the school and were together in the office all day. After a short while, when we became a well-oiled machine, we also socialized along with our husbands, and frequently other members of Gisha's family or close friends. Her friends became my friends. We were as close as a mother and daughter, but with none of the emotional tangles with which that relationship is often fraught.

Gramma and I,
9 months, at her home.

Gisha Berkowitz

Gramma, in one of her
last months of life, holding
her first great-grandchild,
my son, Ajay, 1966.

Molly Baush

Helen Baush, Molly Baush and Mother

Mother wearing the Delta Queen hat she made in a contest
aboard that paddlewheel boat on the Mississippi, during a trip in 1955
with Daddy, Molly Baush, and her mother, Helen Baush.

We remained friends for over 35 years. When Gisha had a stroke and had to be moved south from her dearly loved, large Mt. Airy home into a care facility close to one of her sons, I knew I'd never see her again. When we parted, she still in the hospital in Philadelphia, I told her that I loved her. I emailed her about once a month. One of her sons read my news to her and thanked me frequently for staying in touch. They told me that it meant a great deal to Gisha, although she could not tell me herself. She died at age 89 in 2017, after a lengthy deterioration that was hard on everyone.

I met Helen Smith, a Canadian, on an Elderhostel trip to the Copper Canyon in Mexico in 2008. This was the trip that eventually propelled me to live in Mexico. We first encountered each other on a traffic island at the El Paso airport, waiting for our hotel shuttle to pick us up. We started talking and didn't stop until she died in 2017, although we never saw each again face-to-face after the trip ended. We continued our conversation via infrequent emails, probably about once every other month or so for all those years. Helen was more than 15 years older than I and she was already experiencing trouble with her eyesight when we met. That was probably the first thing we bonded over, as I have had a number of eye problems over the years and had added some new ones with advancing age. We each had private sleeping accommodations on the trip, but we spent every other moment together. The next morning in our El Paso hotel, we had our first meal together, and found that many of the particulars of our lives were similar in spite of our difference in age.

As we aged, Helen moved from her own home into a retirement community and then to another place that provided her more care. Her eyesight continued to fail, but she carried on with gusto and optimism. She became a strong role model for me as someone aging gracefully and living fully in spite of a debilitating condition. She even went on some other Elderhostel trips by herself. She remembered things I had told her were coming up in my life, and asked about trips when I returned, how I came through a medical procedure, and how my children and grandchildren were. She was surrounded by an enormous, supportive family, and I felt so happy when I read that she had gone with this one or that one to someplace special or with the entire brood! As more time passed, I made the font of my emails larger and larger. She eventually became blind. When one of her daughters contacted me by email to tell me about Helen's death, I wept bitterly. We had always hoped to see each other again.

And Molly Baush Hill, who never had any children of her own, became like a mother to me, and probably for the longest time of any of them, including my own. Molly was in my life from the time I was three and a half and our family moved into our large twin house/medical office in East Mt. Airy until she died when I was 72. Molly and her widowed mother, Helen, lived around the corner in an even-larger house with a lovely side yard dominated by a weeping willow tree, which I loved, and a pond— with goldfish even—that intrigued me. As soon as my father hung out his shingle, Helen and Molly became his patients and then friends of our family, playing a lot of bridge and taking trips together. Their favorite was the trip on the Delta Queen, a passenger-carrying steamboat on the Mississippi River, which Molly talked about with me right up to the end. My favorite was when Mother, Daddy, Molly, Helen, and I went to Mexico for several weeks, via New Orleans, leaving my two younger sisters behind with a caretaker. How very adult I felt traveling with them. We had some extraordinary adventures together. I celebrated my 16th birthday in Acapulco on that trip.

Helen and Molly were frequently guests at Dox, rowing our boat, swimming and fishing in the lake, sitting on the patio as evening fell, drinking, talking, laughing, waiting for my father to announce that the grilled chicken was done, and accompanying us to fun places like the Wild Animal Farm.

After Helen died, Molly sold the big house and moved to an apartment, still in the neighborhood. I believe that it was about this time when Daddy decided to give up his general practice and return to school to become a psychiatrist. There was generalized mourning among his patients, none more unhappy than Molly. Although she found another great osteopath to whom she became extremely devoted, in her eyes there was no one like my father.

When my parents moved to West Chester, Pennsylvania, for my father's psychiatric internship, Molly and my parents were separated for the first time. As I had my own household by then, I do not know if the visits between them dwindled, but I have to think that they did. After my parents died, Molly got married for the first time in her 60s. I remember thinking, when I learned of this, that I wanted to run immediately to share this extraordinary news with my parents. They would have been so happy for her. It was probably at this time that I reconnected with Molly, and the older we both became, the closer we got. I loved her and she loved me, and I told her many times that in addition to loving her for herself, I loved her because she had known my parents and we could talk about them and the fun we had had together.

Molly and her husband, Howard, had more than 25

years together, and several years before Molly's death, they moved to a retirement community in the suburbs of Philadelphia and I moved to Mexico. But whenever I was in Philadelphia, they always made it a point to invite me to dinner. When Molly knew she was dying, she went through all of her decades of photos and separated out the ones for her family and for me, from all of the good times our families shared. I was the recipient of color slides, faded black-and-white photos, and a thumb drive with some photos on it, several of which made it into this book. Even at that advanced age, Molly was a techie.

I have learned from personal experience as both a daughter and a mother that the expectations of what a mother is supposed to do and provide are beyond the ability of any one person ever to fulfill. My mother didn't bake, sew, or iron much, but I found other women who did, who were happy to share those skills with me. Mothering is always going on when there is kindness, when time is set aside to be with another person, to listen to her and truly get to know her, to care for her, to protect her, to love her. Attention and caring could come from anyone; it needn't be a woman. I also came to see that while my mother was not able to be everything I needed her to be, and most of all she failed to protect me from my father—but then, she couldn't even protect herself—she *did* give me many things: her great intelligence, her graciousness, her savvy with financial matters, her deep caring for her own mother. I now know that no parent, no mother, no one, can give you everything you need to feel totally loved and protected, that it is your job to seek what you need from others, and that there are always others—and mothers— to provide what you need.

Date unknown
Updated in 2017

WHAT CARLOS TOLD ME
The End of Innocence

Daddy had a college friend, Carlos, with whom I came into more frequent contact, both by mail and by phone, after my father developed Alzheimer's disease and was institutionalized. By the time I was giving Carlos more or less regular updates on Daddy's condition, Carlos was retired and living in Florida, in somewhat reduced circumstances, it seemed to me, and in not particularly great health. I have no idea what work Carlos did before he retired. In fact, looking back, I knew very little about Carlos except that he was my father's friend.

One time, Carlos told me that he wanted to visit my

father before his condition became too advanced. I arranged to put him up in the house adjoining mine since its occupants were away for an extended period of time. Carlos would have his own space, prepare his own meals, and not be disturbed by my family's busy lifestyle, which included two teenagers, Ajay and Suji; two parents working full time; and a German shepherd.

I picked Carlos up from whatever conveyance he used to get to Philadelphia and got him situated in the house next door. I took him shopping for food and invited him for dinner the first night. We had a long talk and Carlos, without any semblance of restraint, mentioned as part of a story that my grandfather—my father's father—had been an alcoholic. He told me this as if I'd always known it. In fact, I hadn't. Daddy was an alcoholic and Mother had been an alcoholic before her death, but I had no idea that my beloved Pop Pop was, too. I searched my memory for evidence, but could find none.

A few days later, Carlos and I were chatting over the back fence, and he told me that my father had had an affair with an old family friend. I couldn't believe it! He told me when and how they met, but I still couldn't picture it. I reeled with this knowledge. I didn't want to know this. I had no need to know this. Why did Carlos tell me this about my father? Was my reluctance to accept this story the usual child's aversion to thinking of her parents as sexual beings? Perhaps. Was it the thought of a woman I'd known well most of my life being with my father—my father, for God's sake!—that blew me away? Upon reflection, I figured that my parents—drowning in booze and in their hate for each other—weren't on good conjugal terms and that this widowed lady was without a partner for a long time.

Then Carlos told me that my father, after my mother's death and when he was beginning to exhibit signs of approaching dementia, showed up on this woman's doorstep, unannounced, all the way from Lebanon, Pennsylvania, at her home many states away. One time Daddy left his suitcase in a motel in which he stayed en route and the woman had to help him sort that out since he couldn't remember the name or location of the motel. That I could readily believe, since he'd set off from his place to mine for an Easter dinner once and wound up God only knows where. A kind fireman called me from a firehouse saying my father was there and confused and could we please come and get him. That was the end of that Easter dinner, as it required two people to rescue him, one to drive our car and one to drive his car back. That was the point when I realized that he could no longer be allowed to drive and that he needed to see a neurologist

109

for a complete work-up.

The diagnosis, as clearly as it could be made without an autopsy, was Alzheimer's. He had to surrender his car keys to the doctor. (Thank you, Doctor, whoever and wherever you are, for taking that burden from me; I'll always be grateful.) And he was transferred directly from the hospital to a nursing home in order to take advantage of a Medicare rule.

I never told Daddy that I knew about his affair. Actually, by the time I found out, he was too far gone. And would I have told him had he not been? No. What would have been the point? I also never told the woman. What would be the point in that discussion, also? I think of her in exactly the same way as I used to; I simply cannot imagine her with my father. I just can't.

One day during Carlos' visit, I collected his laundry, since I didn't want him using a strange washing machine. When I took his things out of my dryer and started to fold them, I noticed some rather unusual underwear. In the front of one pair of briefs was a neatly finished, sizable hole, above which was written, "Eeek, here comes the big wiggly worm." To say I was nonplussed would be to understate my reaction completely. What was this? There were several other equally provocative pairs of underwear in that load of laundry.

Carlos had never married; I knew that. Was he gay? It made no difference to me, of course, but I think I got my answer when, a few days later, he asked me to drive him to an adjacent neighborhood to visit a priest friend of his. I took him before dinner and told him to call me when he wanted me to pick him up. He said there would be no need as he was staying overnight and his friend would bring him back in the morning. Was I driving him to a tryst with a gay priest? Just writing this makes me laugh out loud at myself. I was a relatively innocent 30-something woman learning revelation after revelation about eye-opening topics like family alcoholism, affairs, sex, gay sex. I couldn't take it all in at once. Have I done so even now?

2005

When My Father Died...

When my father died, a nurse from Pine Run, an Alzheimer's facility in suburban Doylestown, called me early in the morning on October 6, 1987, to tell me that Daddy had expired in his sleep at age 71 of pneumonia as a complication of Alzheimer's disease. I immediately asked to speak to his doctor to remind him of what I had put in writing in every document I could think of, that my father was to have a brain autopsy, the only way at that time to determine officially if he indeed had had Alzheimer's. The test results came back positive. Just as the doctor had thought, Alzheimer's was the correct diagnosis.

When my father died, I didn't have to visit Pine Run ever again, as I had so many times since my father became a patient there in 1983. I told the nurse who called to throw away my father's few belongings. The on-file funeral home took over from that point and performed the prearranged services, which included cremation.

About a week later, I answered the door at my home and a man handed me a surprisingly heavy cardboard box, which, he said, contained my father's ashes. After the initial shock and feeling of creepiness wore off, I couldn't resist the temptation to look. In addition to ashes, there were bits of bone. I put the box in a plastic bag in the closet in my office, where it remained until my sisters and I came up with a plan to scatter the ashes. Suji was freaked out by the ashes being in our house.

The ashes did not arrive in time for the small memorial service held at my Unitarian church a few days after he died.

Finally, the next spring, Julia, Gretchen, and I were all able to take time off the same week. We met in Taos, New Mexico, Julia's home, I carrying, probably illegally, the weighty box of ashes in my backpack on the plane. Julia drove us to Ojo Caliente Mineral Springs, where we hiked for a while, I still carrying the ashes. When we came to the Rio Ojo Caliente, I finally and forever physically removed my father from my shoulders. We had all brought something to read aloud; we held hands and cried. Finally, each of us holding a corner of the box, we eased Daddy's ashes into the water and watched as some sank and others were carried away by the current. "Enjoy the journey," I remember saying. We continued to hike, I feeling unburdened and freer than I had for a very long time.

When my father died, I walked around in complete shock when I saw that people on the street just went on about their lives as if nothing had happened, when, in fact, my last parent had just taken his final breath. My overwhelming emotion was an enormous sense of relief. Although Daddy had lived in a series of institutions as his illness worsened, I had taken care of many of his needs for seven years, spending most Sunday afternoons with him, visiting, taking him on long walks, having lunch with him, and helping him to socialize, and in the early years, taking him out to cultural events I thought he would enjoy. I did all of this while working full time and also part time for my husband's business, keeping track of two busy teenagers and a large dog, and maintaining a four-story, five-bedroom house and sizable lawn and garden. I paid my father's taxes and bills, kept track of his investments, and made sure that the places he lived were keeping their side of the bargain. I got no help from any quarter with this crushing burden, and I was under almost unbelievable stress. I put on forty-five pounds.

When my father died, I remember saying out loud to myself, "He can't hurt me anymore." This was odd, though; since he was severely incapacitated by his disease for a long time before his death, he hadn't been able to hurt me in some ways for years. The sight of him at the beginning of his disease, looking so amazingly fit, handsome, and healthy, which physically he was, but not able to string together a coherent sentence nor understand what the hell was happening to him and his mind, certainly hurt me. When he lashed out at me in anger because of what he couldn't remember or do, I was terribly hurt, and when I saw him the next time and knew that he had absolutely no memory of the incident, while I cried and thought of nothing else in the intervening week, I ached with anguish. When the day came that I went to see him and there was no flicker of recognition in his eyes of me as his daughter, I have probably never been more devastated than in that moment. And when he lay, toward the end, skinny and shrunken, in his hospital bed after falling and breaking his hip and was well on his way to dying, the pain that caused me was brutal.

But it was the other kinds of hurt that I meant by that realization and declaration: "He can't hurt me anymore." The unnecessary strictness with a well-behaved daughter. The lack of trust in a trustworthy child. The beating down of my mother emotionally over the years until she was almost not present as herself at all. The undervaluing of the voice of a child until it nearly stilled, not to be awakened again for decades. The extreme control he had over everyone and everything in that house and that family. The stealing of my childhood by forcing me to act the adult when he conceded that role to alcoholism and the resulting bad behavior. The thrall in which he kept people—patients, friends—so that no one ever spoke of the unspeakable, keeping us all in the grip of the big secret. The relentless pressure for perfection from his daughters. The humiliations. The physical punishments, the punishments that outweighed the "crimes" many times over.

When my father died, I was free. When my father died, I could live.

2017

The Philadelphia Inquirer
Wednesday, Oct. 7, 1987

Deaths here

Dr. Anton H. Claus, 71, a retired general practioner and psychiatrist, died yesterday at the Medical Center for the Aging at Doylestown. He was a former resident of East Mount Airy.

A 1941 graduate of the Philadelphia College of Osteopathy, he served with the Navy in Wolrd War II, working in tropical disease control in New Guinea, Australia and Trinidad.

He had been in practice for 25 years when he opened a study of psychiatry at Hahnemann College. He served his residency in psychiatry at Embreeville State Hospital and joined the staff at Philhaven, a Mennonite Hospital in Mount Gretna, Pa. He retired 10 years ago.

Survivors: daughters, Cynthia Meswani, Julia Wood and Gretchen Yarnall, and five grandchildren.

Services: memorial, 11 a.m. Friday, Unitarian Church of Germantown, 6511 Lincoln Drive.

My father's obituary in
The Philadelphia Inquirer.

So intense were this olfactory experience and the feelings
it reawakened in me that I stopped my Thanksgiving dinner
preparations and went immediately to write this story.

Pop Pop's Cigar

Standing in my compact and efficient kitchen on my 54th Thanksgiving, I was cutting up cold yams for a fruited sweet potato casserole. The yams had been baked in the oven the night before, nestled next to the pumpkin pie. As I removed the skins and diced the deep orange flesh, fresh string beans were parboiling on the stovetop next to me. Gently sautéed onions, garlic, and parsley awaited their addition to a Mediterranean vegetable bake. The classic strains of an all-American composers program played softly on public radio. Suddenly, I smelled a familiar acrid odor from my past. And it was as vivid to me as the color of the potatoes in my hand. It was, unmistakably, Pop Pop's cigar.

Pop Pop—my father's father, dead over 30 years. Henpecked and alcoholic (though I didn't know it as a child), he was a gentle soul, happiest in the greenhouse of the flower shop that his mother had owned and that he subsequently ran with his younger brother, John, in a deteriorating section of North Philadelphia. There he reigned—sleeves rolled up, glasses coated with a fine mist of soil, thick white hair spilling over his forehead, stooped over some plant that he tended with his cracked, blackened hands. And always with the cold stub of a cigar clenched in his teeth.

If I was way up in my third-floor bedroom when Pop Pop came over, I could tell immediately that he was in the house. His cigar smell wafted right up those three stories in an instant, and in another instant I would be downstairs wrapped in his earthy hug. Although Mother let him smoke in our house (as there was already plenty of that going on with my parents' heavy cigarette habit), Pop Pop was never allowed to enjoy a cigar in his own home. After a meal at their house, as Grossmama reimposed order in the kitchen and dining area, Pop Pop would silently disappear outside to savor his tobacco.

Holidays were very busy for Pop Pop and the flower business, and Christmas Eve was the busiest. There were Christmas trees and poinsettias to sell, wreaths and centerpieces to construct and deliver. My two grandmothers, Grossmama and Gramma, joined our family around six on Christmas Eve and had dinner

119

before decorating the tree. Pop Pop came straggling in, exhausted, around eight o'clock. He ate leftovers and immediately lay down for a nap on the treatment table in my father's medical office. Later he awoke and joined in the festivities.

Pop Pop sold his share of the flower business to Uncle John and retired, but he never really knew what to do with himself. In the fall, he came over and helped us rake leaves. Shortly after his retirement, the land on which the flower shop stood was condemned for the expansion of Temple University Hospital. Pop Pop drove down to North Philadelphia to watch the wrecking ball demolish his family's lifelong business along with the surrounding row houses of his customers and friends. One month later he was dead of a heart attack on the boardwalk in Ocean City, New Jersey.

As new tears fell from my cheeks onto the yam-smeared knife in my hand, I turned around to see if perhaps someone smoking a cigar had gotten into the house without my knowledge. But by then, the cigar smell had vanished; it couldn't have lasted more than 10 seconds. I sniffed around, trying to recapture it. It was gone. But by its fleeting power, the smell of Pop Pop's cigar had flooded my heart with family memories.

1997

Pop Pop, left, and his brother, my great-uncle John Claus, in front of the
Claus Bros. Florist shop in North Philadelphia.
Note the cigar in my grandfather's left hand.

Greenhouse interior

REGRET II
The Day I Knew

I had been working at The Lutheran Theological Seminary at Philadelphia for 13 years. Much had happened to me, personally and professionally, during that time. When I first applied to the seminary at age 40, it was for the job of faculty secretary. After my interview, it was determined that I was overqualified, and it was recommended that I not take it. Since the seminary was an easy walk from my house, and the job required only 35 hours a week, I was disappointed. But, as things often do, when that door closed, another opened—and at the same institution.

One of the professors who had interviewed me had bought my Gramma's house some years earlier and thus knew me from two vantage points. Several weeks after my rejection, he called to say that a new post had been created—administrative assistant for the newly forming Development Office—and that he thought I would be a good candidate. I applied and got the job. The Development Office was the first at the seminary to be computerized, and I the first employee to get a computer and training on word processing and the creation of a database.

Working with a number of bosses who came and went over the years—even one who, tragically, was murdered—my duties increased as it became obvious that I had the requisite skills. I lent a hand on various of the school's publications, learned all about bulk mailing, and generally proved myself to be an intelligent and reliable worker. When I started to chafe under the routine of the Development Office, it was coincidentally at a time of change at the top of the administration. A much-beloved president retired and a professor of homiletics was elected to that post from within.

The new president, Bob, had known me and my work from our collaboration on a preaching journal. I told him that I thought it was a good time for me to look elsewhere for a job, since I was feeling stifled in the Development Office after so many years, and that there really was nowhere for me to go in the hierarchy of the seminary as it stood then. There were the professors and the directors of about a half-dozen departments, all of whom were Lutheran ministers, and then there were the support personnel. There was no other level to which I could aspire. Plus, I was not Lutheran.

But Bob believed in me and created another level. I became the administrative assistant to the president for publications. In this job, I was the editor of the quarterly alumni/ae journal and managing editor of the preaching journal and of a new publication to address particularly urban ministry. I worked on all admissions materials, including the development of a video for prospective students. I wrote press releases, engaged photographers, and worked with freelance designers. I continued with the Development Office's main work in concert with the director of development—soliciting, receiving, and acknowledging gifts—and I took on the role of personnel officer, overseeing all 13 of the seminary's secretarial staff, hiring and firing as needed, and conducting yearly evaluations along with their supervisors. The new president treated me as a treasured confidante, bouncing ideas and dreams off me, and included me in staff meetings. I worked very hard and felt challenged and appreciated.

When I first came to the seminary, my marriage

of nearly 20 years was fraying. Ajay had already left for college in another city, and our daughter Suji was in her midteens. My father was slowly drifting away into the fog of Alzheimer's disease. With the stress of my job and my home life, I put on weight over the next few years. At my fattest, I decided to leave my husband, and moved out one year after our empty nest proved to be just that. During that first year in my own apartment, I got myself together physically and emotionally while continuing my job. I received support from my seminary colleagues in this whole endeavor, including my divorce.

After a year on my own, I met a man whom I eventually married. Because it was a second marriage, it was just Mario and I, Suji, and the minister for the ceremony. I sent an engraved announcement while on our vacation/ honeymoon to tell the folks at the seminary of our marriage, our new address, and my decision to retain my maiden name. On my return to work, my news could not have been received more lovingly. A big reception was thrown for us some months after the quiet wedding.

But after I had been married for four years and working at the seminary for 13, three very bad things happened one Friday, and I knew I had to leave. I felt as if I had been struck, so stunning were these things—and all at the hands of the same person. I closed my office door that

Friday in a rage and a fog of disillusionment. I sobbed all the way home. I could hardly wait to get in the door to let it all out.

My husband was 15 years older than I and had retired from his job about a year before we were married. He prepared dinner for us every night, and that was a gift in my eyes. I'd had the experience for many years of coming home from a full day's work and immediately diving into dinner preparations for my family, barely having time to change clothes. So I really appreciated those hot meals waiting for me each night.

This particular evening, I crashed through the front door, screaming, "I've been screwed!" I threw down my briefcase, stomped through the dining room, and stood at the kitchen door wailing out my story. Mario was standing at the stove, stirring a big pot of his delicious spaghetti sauce. As I ranted, he never skipped a beat. He didn't turn off the gas; he didn't put down his wooden spoon and come over and throw his arms around me and comfort me. He didn't ask me any questions or offer any comments. He stayed at his post at the stove, stirring methodically, glancing up at me now and then. I stood there in agony, my guts figuratively hanging out of my body, 13 years of hard work and loyalty seemingly counting for nothing, and my husband did not budge! My sense of betrayal was profound. Because of my alcoholic parents, I had felt abandoned emotionally much of my early life, and now here I was again, at a very dark moment, abandoned.

Later that evening, I called the director of admissions at the seminary, a Lutheran minister who was a colleague and friend, and asked if I could talk to him about what had happened. He said that on Sunday, he was having dinner at his daughter's house, not far from mine, and that afterward he would come over and we could talk. We sat on my back porch in the fading summer light while Mario pulled weeds in the front yard, and I spilled out all of my anger and frustration at the sequence of events at the seminary and alluded to the fact that my husband couldn't or wouldn't deal with my fury. In true pastoral style, he listened long and hard. When I told him I felt I had to quit, he understood and didn't try to dissuade me. He gave me some practical pointers on how I should go about it, and he left. He had done his job well; I felt some degree of peace with the seminary situation and my decision to leave.

The following Monday, I submitted my resignation, to take place exactly six months later, on December 31, 1996. My sense of dedication and loyalty was such, even then, that I couldn't leave the seminary abruptly. I needed to make sure that my departure and the filling of my duties were done in an orderly, well-thought-out manner.

And it took me four more years to make my departure from Mario, also in an orderly, well-thought-out manner. Some of the seeds of that separation were sown that summer night in the kitchen as he stirred the sauce but did not stir to attend to his wife in crisis.

2005

Mario L. Minuti
and
Cynthia Claus

are pleased to announce that
they were married in a private ceremony
at the Unitarian Society of Germantown
on August 13, 1992.

After September 9,
they will reside at
2 Betsy Lane
Ambler, PA 19002
(215) 643-2404.

Cynthia will continue to use
her family of origin name.

Mario Minuti's and my wedding announcement card.

Mario and I after our wedding in the Daskam Room of the Unitarian Society of Germantown, in Philadelphia. Rev. Max Daskam, after whom the room was named, had officiated at my parents' wedding.

Mario and I dancing at the wedding reception of my daughter, Suji Meswani, and her husband, Geoff Weiser, at Cliveden, a historical home in Germantown.

THE ELEPHANT IN THE ROOM
A Cautionary Tale for Adults

She would swear, if asked today, that there was not an elephant on the dining room table in either her apartment or his house during the time they were dating.

She knows there was a huge one at her parents' home when she lived there as a child, but she was sure she had been careful to leave it behind when she packed up her things years ago to move out of that house once and for all.

There probably was one on the kitchen table (there was no dining room) when they visited his elderly mother, but it had been easy to overlook since it seemed to be about the size of a sugar bowl. Of course now that she really thinks back, it did tend to grow quite a bit bigger when other family members were also visiting at Thanksgiving or Mother's Day. But so in love were they that she really didn't pay much attention to it.

When they were married and moved into their new house together, she is positive no elephant was in sight. She surely would have noticed it while unpacking the dishes and glasses and candlesticks and placing them carefully in the dining room hutch.

So it's really difficult for her to pinpoint exactly when the elephant first appeared on their own dining room table.

Was it when they discovered they had very different ideas about money? Could it have been when his brother first suggested that it was time to start talking about other living arrangements for their mother? The day she came home from work announcing she was quitting, she clearly saw it out of the corner of her eye as she ranted and raved and he stood impassively stirring the spaghetti sauce.

But she noticed that the elephant really began to have a presence at the dining room table when her husband refused to follow up on some medical test results. Of that she is sure. They'd sit down to dinner and there was the elephant on the lazy Susan that held the napkins, her pill bottles, and the little pitcher of milk for their coffee. It seemed to grow very fast once it got firmly situated at the dining room table, and within a month, they had to push the elephant's trunk or leg aside in order to put their plates down to eat.

One day it had grown so large that they couldn't see each other over its bulk. They could still talk to each other, of course, if they raised their voices, but soon it became too much of an effort, and pretty soon they stopped talking to each other at dinnertime.

Then one night, to her horror, she discovered the elephant in their bed. When they got in and slipped under the covers and turned to nuzzle each other goodnight, there it was on the pillow between their heads. So they didn't kiss each other goodnight, but they were content to have their hips and legs and toes touching in the dark warmth of the bed.

But little by little, the elephant grew in the bed, too, until they could no longer touch each other at all. Even in their queen-sized bed, they found themselves on the very opposite edges, almost falling off. They would call "good night" to each other over the elephant, but soon they gave that up, too.

After being confined to the dining room table and the bed for some time, the elephant began to take over the rest of the house. Any time they tried to sit in the same room to read or watch television, the elephant would muscle its way between them, forcing them to sit in separate rooms.

There was no way they could carry on a conversation when they were in separate rooms.

Then came the day when they returned from an errand and discovered that they could not get back into their house. The elephant's head was bursting out the front door, its legs were sticking out of the first-floor windows, and even its tiny tail was out the kitchen door and lying on the screened-in porch. Its mass had crushed everything in the house and ruined it. They could not live there together anymore.

They moved into separate apartments.

A little while later, when she went to meet the real estate agent they had hired, she was surprised to find the house in perfect condition. There was no damage and no elephant in sight. The front door was back on its hinges and the windows were no longer broken. She was so glad to see the house looking normal. She wanted to tell him about it, but it was much too late; they weren't speaking to each other anymore.

Date unknown

May 15, 2011

Dear Larry,

You cannot imagine the time and energy I put into choosing what I would wear to our 50th high school reunion today. I ordered four pairs of silver sandals from Zappo's so I could select the perfect ones and return the others. I meticulously timed my haircut in order to look my best. And I lost 10 pounds. Ever since I learned—way last December—that such a reunion would take place, I had been thinking of meeting up with you again. When I received my invitation that included the list of "missing" students, I quickly scanned the B's, and was happy to see that your name wasn't there.

During the final week before the big day, I had trouble sleeping a couple of nights, as I lay in bed fantasizing about how our meeting would go, what I would open with, how you would respond. Would we go someplace else together afterwards? Would we still be attracted to each other? I wanted to see if it was true what is said about meeting old sweethearts at reunions, how often the old spark is still there and a very intense relationship can spring up again. Or, would you bring a wife?

I was in quite a state by the time today rolled around. A certain calm came over me, though, as I drove to the restaurant, parked the car, and entered the hall. I got my nametag, raffle ticket, and goodie bag, and plunged into the crowd. I didn't see you immediately. I knew you'd be easy to spot because of your height. Then I thought I saw you. I went over quickly to what must be your doppelganger, a guy named Reinhold according to his nametag, whom I didn't remember at all. He tricked me a bit with his height and, when he lowered his head to hear me better, his tobacco breath. But it was not you. In my distracted state, I met Martin, with shoulder-length gray curls, walking with difficulty on crutches. I remembered that he had had polio. He was accompanied by a beautiful, younger wife, who was sweet and attentive to him. And Walter, who had brought his grown daughter, shared a photo of his twin sister, Emily, who had died of ovarian cancer. As I kept scanning the room, I was beginning to fear that you weren't there.

I stumbled into Marnie, a classmate through all 12

years of school, and she invited me to sit at her table where several other friends—Carol and Lois, whom I'd also known since the first grade—were seated, along with some husbands. It was a comfortable group, as I soon learned that I was not the only divorcee. We were being urged to sit, but I didn't stop looking for you.

Welcoming remarks were made and people began to file up to the buffet by table. While waiting, I flipped through the program booklet. I glanced at the names of the reunion committee, skipped over some doggerel "In Honor of the Germantown High School Class of June 1961 50th Class Reunion," ignored many pages of memories with a "space left blank to add a few of your own," and then sped through a nine-page listing of all those graduates the committee had found, with an asterisk next to those present. You were not listed. My heart sank. Where were you? Finally, on the very last page, I saw about three dozen names under the heading "In Memorium," and that's where I found you. Your last name was spelled incorrectly by the addition of an extra letter, and I held out a moment of ridiculous hope that there might be someone in the class with that name. A quick check of Marnie's copy of our yearbook, however, proved that a typo doesn't undo a fact. You were dead. I couldn't take that concept in. This was not a possibility

I had ever considered. I felt ill. The sounds in the room disappeared and I just sat there, stupefied.

In shock, I held it together through the somewhat-cheesy program and the photo session until I got out into my car for the ride home. Once I was safely alone, I allowed myself to express all of the pent-up nervous energy and hopes for our private reunion and dreams of what we might have meant to each other now, and the tears began to fall.

When I got home, I craved more information about your death to make it more real to me than a listing on a page: when and why at such a young age? I called our friend Art, who said that you had succumbed to lung cancer even before our 40th reunion. He didn't know anything else. I guess you never gave up the smoking.

I had longed to meet the man that you had become. I wanted to tell you of my life—about my children and grandchildren, my work and my retirement—and I yearned to hear about yours. Where were you living? What kind of work did you do? Had you retired? Were your parents still living? How and where was your sister who had the same name as mine? And most important, did our relationship mean as much to you as it did to me?

I wondered if you remembered events the same way I did—like me popping in to visit you at work on a Saturday afternoon in your father's shop and being warmly welcomed by him. Like the enormous amount of time we spent together, from early in the morning, when you'd drive way out of your way to pick me up for the ride to school in time for my before-school majorette practice. Like us never having a fight, never breaking up and getting back together again, no drama. I remember a comfortable, easy-going relationship that made room for others, your friends and mine. Was that your memory of us, too?

You and I were in all the same accelerated academic classes, and after school, we hung out. We dated on the weekends. Surely you never forgot all the times we drove down to Valley Green to "park." Do you remember my "make-out clothes," those shorts and that blouse I kept in your car to change into before the kissing and petting began, so I could return home wearing the same starched and ironed blouse and skirt I started out in, completely unruffled? I don't remember making the actual changeover before or back again when it was time to go. Did I modestly get into the backseat to do it?

And who could forget my 11 p.m. curfew and the consequences if I came in late? We kept an eye on our watches all the time we were out, and you were so cooperative and helpful in getting me home on time. You never acted put-out because of the somewhat-early hour I had to return home, and other stupid rules I lived with, and in hindsight, I deeply appreciate that. There was that one awful time, when your front tires went over the concrete barrier at the parking lot and we couldn't back up to drive away. After a quick conference, we decided that we'd knock on the steamed-up window of the car next to us, throw ourselves on their mercy, and ask them to drive me home. A miracle—they agreed. You accompanied me home and then they drove you back to your car, where you dealt with a AAA tow truck that you had called from a pay phone somewhere along the way.

And you let me drive your car! You helped me practice my driving in preparation for my driver's test. That showed such faith in me. Do you remember the time you were teaching me the finer points of working the clutch and the accelerator, and I took off in first gear like a shot with smoking, squealing tires? I don't know which of us was more surprised!

Do you remember attending both our junior and senior proms together? I felt so beautiful in my full-length strapless gown of silvery blue, and you looked handsome in a white dinner jacket with a boutonniere. I'm grateful that there is a photo of us in our yearbook dancing in a conga line at the prom, having the time of our lives.

As you well know, we never made love fully, although it was not for your lack of trying nor my lack of desire for you. The closest we ever came was at the graduation party you hosted in the community room of your apartment building. I clearly remember exactly what I wore, a black-and-white checked dress and red high heels, especially since I took them all off. We were in the quarters of the apartment's handyman next door, and I remember tangled limbs on his bed, but then he knocked on the door and shouted that he wanted us to get out. I was saved by that interruption, as I wasn't ready yet at age 17 for that final step.

You know, Larry, I saw you twice in those 50 years. You and your wife and children moved into a house around the corner from where I lived with my husband and children. I don't know how I knew you lived there—perhaps I saw you in the yard—but on Halloween, with my heart in my throat, I took my children to trick-or-treat at your house. They were not the only ones I dressed with care that night. I wanted to look good to you. You answered the door and we greeted each other warmly; that's all I remember. Later, I heard somehow that you had been divorced, as I was. And then, probably not so long before you died, as I now figure it, I was two or three customers behind you in a checkout line at Kmart in Flourtown, close enough to reach out and touch you. You were buying an inexpensive charcoal grill. You had aged, of course, but I would have known that tall, slightly stooped profile and your voice anywhere. I don't know why, but I didn't call out your name. It was the last time I ever saw you.

Maybe it was because by then, I was remarried. Maybe I didn't feel good about my appearance and what I was wearing that day for a quick errand to Kmart. Maybe because it was you who broke up with me on that Thanksgiving Day of freshman year in college. I had foolishly made my college choice so as to be somewhat near you, and we did actually manage to get together once in the first couple of months and it was joyous, but arrangements were difficult. I remember that while I was home for the first time over that long weekend, I drove my mother's Pontiac to the annual football rivalry between Germantown and Roxborough, although we hadn't planned on meeting there. I sensed from your letters that things were cooling off between us, so I was hoping you'd be there. And then I remember driving home, sobbing, and my mother saying quietly, a little later in the day, "Did you and Larry break up?" Yes, you broke up with me.

I wonder if you would have attended the reunion if you were still alive. I don't know you well enough now to have

141

a sense of what the answer would be to that. All I know is that I loved you once, and I deeply love my memories of you and what you brought to my life. And I think you demonstrated in a hundred small ways that you loved me, too. I don't think that any other romantic relationship that I've had was quite as relaxed and natural as it was with you. Although many speak of the agonies of their high school years, I loved mine, and I'm sure your presence in them went a long way toward making them so happy.

Rest in peace,

Cynthia

CYNTHIA LOUISE CLAUS
731 Vernon Road   Academic
Majorettes 10B, 11A, 11B, 12A, 12B; F.T.A.
11B; Lunchroom Aide 11B; Monitor 10A, 10B;
A.A. Representative 10A; Clipper Reporter
11B, 12A, 12B; Yearbook Literary Editor 12B;
Slide Rule Club 12A, 12B.
Although no relation to Santa, "Cindy" has
the same jolly nature. During the fall term,
she may be seen twirling a baton at our football games. Cindy plans to enter the field of
education after her graduation from college.
May success be her reward.

*My page from the Revidere, the yearbook of Germantown High School,
Philadelphia, from which I graduated in 1961.*

Literary Editors:
M. Stroup, C. Claus

*Marnie Stroup and I as co-literary
editors of our 1961 yearbook.*

*Larry Benner, my boyfriend
in high school.*

*I in my high school majorette outfit and line-up.
I'm the fifth from the right, wearing glasses.*

Larry and I as part of a conga line at our senior prom,
spring 1961. We are just left of center.

The Slide Rule Club of Germantown High School, 1960-61. Perhaps
because Larry was in the club (fourth from left), I was the only girl.

Larry and I at the Sweetheart Ball (third couple from the right), 1960.

IN MEMORIUM

We pause to remember our classmates who have passed away all too soon
and who have left us with wonderful memories

Phyllis Anderson	Daniel Kelman
Anthony Bassetti	Sue Kornblatt
Robert Ball	Bonnie Kurland
Louise Baumeister	Bart Landauer
Robert Beale	Isaac Lane
Larry Brenner	Mark Lempert
Michael Brockmon	Susan McKeon (McCormick)
Arnold Brown	Barbara Mielziner
Henry Chestnut	Sheila Muchnick
Deborah Dashefsky (Margolis)	Emilie Pouch
Susan Drill (Avedor)	Diane Powers (Bennis)
Ronald Floyd	Marc Rosenbluth
Elaine Galfand	Howard Rosenfeld
James Gill	Stephen Selkow
Muriel Gilman	David Schanzer
Steve Goldman	Laraine Singer
Herman Grady	Marlyn Smith (Stansbury)
Shirley Ann Hicks	Florence Szymanski(Podulka)
Harry Houston	Robert VanBriggle
Albert Hutchins	Bernard Montgomery Vanhorn
Cynthia Jackson	Taazmayia Waters
Alan Johnson	Lloydine Mary White
Thomas Johnson	Thomas Williams
Richard Jones	

*The In Memorium page from the program of the 50th reunion
of Germantown High School, Class of 1961.
Larry's name, with the misspelling crossed out by me,
is the sixth one down on the left.*

Page 10   CHESTNUT HILL LOCAL   Thursday, June 16, 2011

A group of former Chestnut Hill residents in the J.S. Jenks School graduating class of 1957 attended a recent gathering for the 50th anniversary of Germantown High School's class of 1961 (from left): Mary Schmeidel (Psichos) of Centennial Colo., Merrie Lawson (Rowan) of Whittier, N.C., Lois Wettstone (Nelson) of Pleasant Valley, Va., Lance Horowitz of Meadowbrook, Pa., Myrnie McLaughlin (Stroup) of Salisbury, N.C., Carol Flavell (Massaro) of Dedham, Mass. and Cynthia Claus of Philadelphia.

*A photo from the Chestnut Hill Local of June 16, 2011,
taken at my 50th high school reunion.*

145

Christmas Story

1951

I am eight years old and still believe in Santa Claus. It is Christmas Eve and Grossmama is over for dinner, a quickly thrown-together meal, hurriedly eaten in order to get to the main events of the day. There is much to do! Pop Pop will arrive later. He is still at the flower shop, selling the last of the wreaths and trees, and seeing to the delivery of the final poinsettias and centerpieces for the tables of tomorrow's feasts. While Grossmama entertains my six-years-younger sister, Julia, my mother washes up the dinner dishes and continues preparations for their traditional Christmas Eve open house, which begins in a few hours. Daddy and I rearrange the living room to accommodate the Christmas tree. Then we go out to the cellarway to attach the stand and bring it in. When the tree is wrestled into place, everyone gathers to ooh and aah, to sniff deeply at the pine scent, and to offer an opinion on the tree's "best side."

Next it's a trip to the cellar to haul up the huge cardboard box filled with decorations. When it's opened, and the contents spread out on a card table, it's like seeing old friends who appear ever so briefly only once a year—the jointed construction paper Santa with the cotton ball beard that my father made in kindergarten; the antique blown glass balls that had come over with my great-grandparents from Germany; impossibly twisted lengths of cord from colored lights; baked dough ornaments, slightly chipped and moldy; tiny stockings with our names spelled out in glitter. And look, there is the green felt tree skirt on which we'll nestle the little village at the base of the tree. There's that chicken with only one leg that won't stand up anymore. We should throw it away, but we never do.

We have a time-honored sequence for the placing of the decorations on the tree. My job is to untangle the light cords and screw in the bulbs. When I plug them in and they all light up, everyone cheers. Meanwhile, Daddy anchors the tree to the wall with wire and nails. When the lights are affixed and bulbs exchanged so no two of the same color are next to each other, everybody starts decorating the tree. While standing on a stepstool, my father hangs the tiniest balls from the spindliest top branches. As the branches grow thicker, the balls get larger and weightier. Then the miscellaneous objects are strategically placed. The final step is to lay tinsel strips over the finished product. Then it is up onto the stepstool again for the crowning touch—the angel on the highest branch. We plug in the lights again and stand back to admire our handiwork.

Open boxes, tissue paper, ornament hangers, pine needles, and chips of cardboard litter the living room floor, but I am Cinderella at the ball, and it is nowhere near midnight. As we clean up, Mother brings out Christmas cookies and eggnog. Every year Grossmama gets a little tipsy, or pretends to, and dons Christmas-tree ball earrings and dances around the living room.

Julia is put to bed and I have the honor—and terror—of putting out a snack for Santa. It has gotten late, and I live in mortal fear that Santa will arrive before I am safely asleep. I quickly place the plate with the liverwurst and mustard on rye next to the bottle of beer, hang everybody's stockings at the fireplace nearby, and with kisses all around, fairly fly to bed.

The next morning, Julia and I wake our parents hideously early. Their open house had lasted until the wee hours and they are very tired. After marveling that Santa actually ate the snack we left for him, and even wrote a thank-you note, we open the gifts in our stockings and then have breakfast—always *brioche* on Christmas morning. Then it is on to the opening of the big presents. My God, it is an embarrassment of riches by anyone's standards. With two doting grandmothers, dozens of my father's patients who have become our extended family, and lots of relatives in spite of the fact that my parents are both only children, we girls have gifts to open until we are almost bored of it. But that is just the morning; much more awaits us.

The turkey is in the oven. The newly opened presents are stacked neatly under the tree to make room to fully unfurl the dining room table. My grandparents arrive. We girls change from bathrobes and fuzzy slippers to beautiful party dresses and slippery Mary Janes. We pose, twirl, and smile for the cameras. Uncle Wilbur and Aunt Alice arrive. When Uncle Wilbur has had some drinks, he loosens his false teeth in his mouth somehow and clicks them like castanets, accompanied by the singing of others. We are delighted. I sit on Pop Pop's lap while he sings to me in German, "O, Susannah." We give presents to our grandparents and watch mystified and embarrassed as Gramma breaks into tears over her gift of a framed photo of the two of us in matching dresses.

And then comes dinner. The table fairly groans with

the delicious excess of it all. We eat, drink, laugh, and sing. After overseeing weeks of Christmas preparations, an open house, a huge elaborate meal, plus the unbelievable chaos of plenty that is our family's Christmas morning experience, my mother collapses. This is the signal for an annual Christmas ritual: my father and his father, both in aprons, Pop Pop with a cigar in his mouth, wash, dry, and put away all the dishes, glassware, and silverware, and scour the mammoth greasy roasting pan while my exhausted mother relaxes with her guests in the living room. I think the two men enjoy themselves immensely! When things quiet down, we watch Gian Carlo Menotti's *Amahl and the Night Visitors* on television. I see Pop Pop brush away tears as he watches it, the only time I ever saw him cry.

1966

I am 23 years old with a husband of 18 months, Suresh, and a six-month-old baby boy, Ajay. It is Ajay's first Christmas. We have been at my parents' home since about six o'clock to celebrate Christmas Eve with them and my sisters. While three of my grandparents are still alive, one is ill with cancer, and all feel it will be too dangerous for them to drive home later because of a major snowstorm, so they have decided not to come, even for Christmas Eve together. After we have dinner and decorate the tree, the snow has really begun to pile up, and we say we must leave while we still can. We say goodnight to my sisters, who go to their rooms. But Mother offers that we should stay the night, all three of us sleeping on the third floor in the double bed that had been mine not too many years earlier. Ajay is exhausted from all of the attention and stimulation, and we go upstairs at about nine. Mother brings me one of her nightgowns. Suresh says he'll sleep in his underwear. Ajay is already in the pajamas that I had brought with us, as I thought he would fall asleep on the ride home and we could just put him right to bed.

We have been asleep for about an hour when I am awakened by my father's heavy footsteps coming up the stairs. The sound immediately throws me back to my childhood, when I had this bedroom, across the hall from Aunt Gertie's small apartment. It never meant anything good when I heard Daddy's footfalls continue beyond the second floor. The steps from the first to the second floor are carpeted, so that the patients in the waiting room of my father's medical office on the other side of the wall from our living quarters don't hear the whole family thundering up and down. The steps from the second to the third floor, however, are not carpeted, and Daddy's footsteps were terrifyingly loud, strong, and rapid, then as now, as he always took two at a time.

When I heard that sound as a young teenager, I would frantically glance around my room to see if things were reasonably tidy. Bed made? Check! Dirty clothes in the hamper? Happily, yes! Piles of stuff on the floor? Oh my God, yes! My heart would pound, my palms were clammy; I was afraid of what was to come. I would try to guess why he might be coming all the way up to the third floor.

One Halloween, I went to a friend's house after school and was invited to stay for dinner and go trick-or-treating with her that evening. Since I already had my costume with me for the parade and party at school earlier, it wouldn't cause anyone any trouble for me to stay. When I called home to get permission, I was told that I must return home immediately as I had not made my bed that morning. Only by going up to the third floor would my father have known this. Another time, I came home from school and went to my room to discover that Daddy had thrown my entire collection of Archie comic books into the outside trash. I had bought them all, one by one, for 10 cents apiece with part of my allowance over many, many months, and I enjoyed reading them to relax, but my father felt that they were inferior reading material and he ditched them.

Daddy is knocking loudly on the door of the bedroom and then immediately opens it without being invited in. I wonder what awful emergency there must be to cause this behavior. But then I see that he is very drunk and extremely angry. He shouts, "Why are you sleeping here? This is my house and you have a perfectly good house of your own to sleep in. I want you to go home NOW!" At this point, Mother is also outside our door, crying and trying to calm my father, emphasizing the dangerous road conditions outside. He is having none of it. I realize that we had better do as he says. We get dressed and I pick up Ajay and wrap him in blankets, and we sit in the car while it warms, as Suresh cleans off the piles of snow all over it, which takes quite a long time. Mother is watching us from a window. I can see how upset and humiliated she is, but I know she is unable to do anything in the face of my father's unreasonable, drunken wrath. We drive at a snail's pace, slipping and sliding the mile or so to our apartment, and have a very hard time finding a parking space. I keep wondering what my husband is thinking about my father and this insane situation. I think of my sisters, who, I am absolutely sure, could not sleep through the tirade, but stay silent and awake in their beds. I call Mother as soon as we get into the house to reassure her that we have arrived safely.

153

Christmas morning arrives. Streets are difficult if not impassable, and so we have an excuse to beg off going back there to dinner. I feel so sorry for my mother, after her weeks of preparation and all of the food that must be in the house for the holiday dinner, and having to face that dinner alone with Daddy and my sisters. I cannot be with my father on this Christmas Day under any circumstances.

1968

I am 25 years old and my husband and I have found a way to avoid having to deal with Christmas: We go away, far away. One year we had Christmas dinner in an Indian restaurant in Tel Aviv and another year in a Japanese restaurant on Waikiki. It's an ideal solution. Because you're going away, you don't have to have a tree or any other Christmas decorations. Oh, I send Christmas cards; I bake hundreds of elaborate Christmas cookies, mostly to give away. But I don't believe in the main event of the holiday and my husband is from a culture that doesn't celebrate Christmas.

This year, we're making a trip to India, my husband's first visit home since he came to the United States about seven years ago. He is returning with an American wife and a two-year-old son. We will be there for two months. We have planned to be with family in Hyderabad in south India on Christmas Day. Of course there are no Christmas decorations in the streets nor in my husband's cousin's home, as they are Hindus. But they know that it is "my" Christmas Day, and they want to make it festive for me. Almost the moment we arrive, the discussions begin about the special treat they have planned for us for dinner— toasted cheese sandwiches. Instead of the exotic and delicious Indian food that I regularly prepare and eat at home and have grown to love, the family has bought white bread and some kind of cheese and a machine somewhat like a flat waffle iron that toasts and compresses the sandwiches. There are about 10 people living in the house, plus us, so making toasted cheese sandwiches in this manner for that many people takes a very long time.

While the preparations are going on, one of the cousins, who my husband told me earlier is a religious fanatic and quite unstable, whisks Ajay away to go for a motor scooter ride through the city. There is no such thing as a helmet in Hyderabad in 1968. They do not return for a very long time and I am frantic. But they do eventually return safely, and Ajay is obviously enchanted with his outing. Then, all 13 of us sit tightly around a small kitchen table with a staggering pile of toasted cheese sandwiches in the middle.

All eyes are on me, as this meal has been prepared in my honor. The purchase of the toasting machine, the foreign white bread and cheese, items the Indians never eat, are a gift to me on my Christmas holiday. I look around at all the people and smile and thank them and wish them a merry Christmas, and then I reach for a toasted cheese sandwich.

1983

I am 40 years old. It is two days before Christmas. My mother died of lung cancer two years ago at the age of 64. Daddy is in a nursing home suffering from advanced Alzheimer's disease. My husband and I and our two children will be leaving in three days for one of our Christmas escape trips.

A few days ago, I received a call from the administrator of my father's nursing home. It was the call I'd been dreading. My father had deteriorated beyond the stage at which the home was willing to have him as a patient. In spite of the Haldol he was on, he was abusive to the other patients and had taken to urinating in the potted plants. I was told that his doctor had made arrangements to admit him to the Alzheimer's unit at Pine Run in Doylestown, a good 60 minutes from my home. I didn't really have any choice in the matter; it was clear they were throwing him out. Christmas and our trip were almost upon us, a trip not to be canceled easily. I agreed to the move.

On the morning of Christmas Eve, his private nurse and I load Daddy and his few belongings into my car and drive the hour to Pine Run. It's a long hour. My father doesn't really talk much anymore, and the nurse is a virtual stranger to me. I crank up the radio playing Christmas music and that isn't bad. I get my father admitted, settled in his room, and unpacked. I am urged by the nursing staff to make a fairly rapid exit and to return the next day. His nurse and I drive back in almost total silence.

Now it is Christmas Day and I arise early. Everyone else is still sleeping. There is no reason for them to get up early; we are not celebrating Christmas. I drive to Doylestown once again and take the elevator to the fifth floor. I go directly to my father's room, but it is empty. I inquire of my father's whereabouts at the nurses' station. I tell the nurse his name, and she starts to laugh. "When they told us from admissions that we were getting a Mr. Claus on Christmas Eve, we thought it was a joke." "*Dr.* Claus," I assert. "He's a doctor…*was* a doctor."

I am directed to a large sunny day room at the end of the hall. As I get closer, I can hear Christmas carols being played on a piano and a woman's voice singing. I enter the room and see Daddy sitting in a chair, looking forlorn and lost. He is not alone. There are perhaps a dozen other patients, most worse off than he. Most are tied into wheelchairs and are nodding off in the overheated room. Several mumble or shout. None are singing or even appear to know that a piano is being played. I get a chair and sit next to my father. I give him the box of Christmas cookies I'd brought for him. I have to open the box for him. I have to hand him a cookie and guide his hand to his mouth so that he will taste the cookie. He has forgotten what cookies are for. I try to sing the carols with the nurse, but I just can't.

Soon it is lunchtime and Daddy is taken to another room where, I am told, the higher-functioning patients eat. A tray of food is set before him. It is Christmas dinner— turkey with all of the trimmings, and a half-pint of milk. It smells delicious. Daddy sits and stares at it. I put the fork and knife in his hands. He sits still, clutching the cutlery. I realize that he does not know what the food is or what he is supposed to do with it. I cut the meat into small pieces, open up the milk container and take the paper off the straw. I put the straw into the container and hold it to my father's lips. He does nothing. I begin to feed him. That goes pretty well. When he is finished, I go to the nurses' station to tell them that my father will have to take his meals in the room with the patients who need to be fed or he will starve to death.

1991

I am 49 years old. My children are grown and long since gone from my house. Suji will spend Christmas visiting India with her father; Ajay is in school in Denmark and has not come home for Christmas for several years. I have been divorced and am remarried. It is my first Christmas with my new husband, Mario. We are going to spend it with his 86-year-old mother in Glen Lyon in upstate Pennsylvania in coal country, a sad little town that shut down when the mines did. We will drive the two hours to her house on Christmas morning and spend a couple of days with her. Mario will give his mother a check, as he does every year. I have earlier sent her a basket of citrus fruit, so no presents will be exchanged. Dreading the bleakness of the occasion, I confide to Mario as we drive that I will have to work very hard this day not to be depressed. "Christmas is just another day," he tells me. He has had lots of practice living that belief. He lost both his only child, an adult son, and his first wife to cancer, 18 months apart, several years ago. He's gotten through every Christmas since then by viewing it as "just another day."

We eat a midafternoon dinner. My mother-in-law has made her traditional *cappelletti* soup and has roasted a small chicken. We decide just to eat in the kitchen and not even bother with the good dishes and silver. After dinner, we play several hours of pinochle around the kitchen table. Then we watch some television and have my mother-in-law's fabulous *zuppa Inglese* for dessert, another family tradition. My mother-in-law is tired from all of her cooking and goes to bed early. Mario and I go out for a walk to get some air and some exercise and to see all the Christmas decorations in the town. They don't have much in Glen Lyon, but they do have the Christmas spirit. In the dark, with the lights twinkling from every house in unbelievably gaudy and mismatched displays, you can't see the boarded-up storefronts. I know we did the right thing by spending Christmas with a woman who probably won't see many more. I know we brought a measure of joy to her. But I am glad the day is almost over, because Christmas is not just another day.

And now for something
totally different!

Addict!

Let me make my confession: I am an addict. With all the possible addictions out there, and the ones peculiar to my family—alcohol, tobacco, nasal inhalers— my addiction seems pretty tame, but it is an addiction no less. I am addicted to ChapStick. I settled on ChapStick after a long history of trying other lip glosses or lip balms. I was for a while inseparable from ChapStick Petroleum Jelly Plus, in the bright yellow tube with angled application—99% white petroleum. No one ever said what the other—"Plus"—1% was. But I often had trouble finding this brand in the drugstore and would become quite agitated until I could locate something equally satisfying. I've used higher-priced tinted glosses and glosses with UV protection, and I even reached bottom once when I bought the CVS generic look-alike.

Years ago, when I regularly wore lipstick, that would suffice during the day. But at night, the last thing I did before retiring was to apply ChapStick. I had to have something greasy on my lips at all times. Now that I rarely wear lipstick, I wear ChapStick 24/7. When I was early in my relationship with my second husband, he noticed that I frequently applied ChapStick and told me he couldn't see any difference between how my lips looked with ChapStick and without. He entirely missed the point! It isn't about how it *looks*; it's all about how it *feels*!

I cannot have naked lips. They quickly dry out and feel like potato chips—or how your lips feel after eating salty potato chips—causing me to lick them constantly. This, of course, leads to even drier lips.

Like all addictions, this is a physiological need. My body requires the greasiness of ChapStick on my lips all the time or I begin to be uncomfortable. This discomfort can be relieved easily by a quick, sometimes surreptitious application of ChapStick. At all times there is a tube in my left pants or skirt or coat pocket and/or in my pocketbook. Of course there is also one in my traveling cosmetics bag, along with several in my bathroom medicine cabinet. If I cannot find a tube or if I'm driving and I can't dig into my pocket under the seat belt to retrieve the ChapStick, I begin to panic and cannot think of anything else until my lips have been coated.

Some years ago, I read Margaret Atwood's frightening look at a possible future, *The Handmaid's Tale*. In it, Offred is a handmaid—a fertile woman forced to bear children for elite barren couples—who is assigned to the household of The Commander and his wife. The Commander becomes enamored of Offred and asks if there is anything he can secretly get for her. The only thing she desires is hand lotion—and fragrance-free hand lotion at that. She could have asked for almost anything, but all she wanted was hand lotion. I totally understood. Had I been in that position, I would have asked for a dozen or so tubes of ChapStick. In fact, I generally buy ChapStick in lots of at least six at a time. And if there is a sale—watch out!

I have told my daughter that when I am old and feeble in the nursing home, strapped into a wheelchair, I want only two things—what I call the necessities of life—tissues and a tube of ChapStick, readily accessible, and I'm totally serious. I know I can depend on Suji to provide me with these things because, you see, she is a lip gloss junkie, also. This insidious addiction has now claimed its second generation! Suji has expanded her drug of choice to include little pots of grease with fancy names and inflated prices, into which you have to dip your finger and then smear it on your lips, but it's really just petroleum jelly in a gussied-up disguise.

Once, at a dinner party, I observed another woman at the table applying ChapStick after the meal and told her that I was about to do the same thing (eating, of course, removes it). We got into a long discussion about our addiction and she told me that there is a web page for ChapStick addiction: *www.LipBalmAnonymous.com.* I could hardly wait to go online and see this site. Little did I know that when I entered the words "lip gloss addiction" in the search engine, up would pop hundreds and hundreds of websites devoted to this need. Some touted a conspiracy theory, talking about an "industry of addiction" or "a ChapStick conspiracy," saying that some lip gloss products actually exfoliate lip skin, causing lips to be dry, thus necessitating an application of lip balm, and round and round the cycle goes. Other sites spoke of support groups with catch phrases such as "Ban the Balm!"

Since these sites say that the first step toward solving the problem of an addiction is admitting that you have one, I am hopefully on the road to recovery by means of this confession. But because it is thought by the medical community that this habit is created by inadvertent lip licking, and in my case, exacerbated by acid reflux disease, I fear it will be a monkey on my back for the rest of my days.

2004

And finally, a poem.

The Piano Lesson

I sat on blond wood,
legs swinging, feet not touching at first,
back ramrod straight
for one long hour a day for six youthful years.

I stared at blobs of ink dancing amid tiny lines,
and other cryptic symbols now my own,
squinting at my first sight of Italy—
pianissimo, forte, adagio, andante moderato.

With clean hands—always clean hands—and nails cut short,
I made the notes rise and sing—
Rachmaninoff, Handel, Schubert, Haydn,
show tunes, waltzes, marches, jigs.

I hated it, of course—
that daily hour stolen from my youth.
Raging fever no excuse to shirk
the laying on of hands to keys of black and white.

But every now and then,
after the obligatory scales were scaled,
and when in spite of myself, the music touched my soul,
from downstairs came appreciation for my toil—applause!
And on rare occasion, Daddy would shout "Bravo!"

Two teachers, so different,
through the years gave their all to me,
even if I returned less than that to them.
The first, Miss Massa, an aged stereotype—her parlor chairs
had antimacassars—
would bribe performance with gummed stars and a drawer
full of Cracker Jack prizes.

The other, her name now gone, but visage clear,
came to the house in camel hair and pumps.
A young, blond beauty, she seemed to float in regally and
transported bespectacled prepubescent me.

On occasion, Daddy and I would play four hands,
mine racing to match his skill and speed,
no love of music possible, overwhelmed
by fear of not doing it right—and of him.

And now?
Now I sit before a new keyboard with a computer chip brain.
Organ thrall? Harpsichord? String quartet? Can do!
And best of all, I can play and no one has to listen—save me.

But as I slide onto the bench and crease the music back
and with clean hands prepare to play anew,
I see his smile, I feel his love, I hear applause.
Bravissimo!

Date unknown

170

The Photos Behind
Other Stories

My father with his three daughters,
from left, Julia, Gretchen, and Cynthia, 1952.

The Claus girls, from left, Cynthia, Gretchen, and Julia, 1953.

The Claus girls, from left, Julia, Gretchen, and Cynthia, 1965.

Mother with me and baby Julia, 1949.

Julia, about 3 years old, 1952.

Gretchen, 14 years old, 1967.

My mother, Eleanor Elizabeth Boal, age 24-25, in 1938 or '39.

Santa's Cousins

Official photo that appeared, along with an article, in The Evening Bulletin *of November 18, 1952, showing all of the children named Claus in the city of Philadelphia holding a key to be presented to our "cousin" Santa Claus at the annual Gimbel's Thanksgiving parade the following week. I am the tall one.*

Julia, left, and I, with our official badges and in our special viewing seats for the 1952 Gimbel's Thanksgiving parade, where later we, along with several other children named Claus (no relation), presented the key to the City of Philadelphia to Santa Claus, who made an appearance at the end of the parade.

The actual article and photo, as explained on preceding page.

Acknowledgments

My heartfelt thanks...

To recently found cousin Liz Claus, for the photo of my grandfather and his younger brother, John, her uncles, outside of Claus Bros. Florists, North Philadelphia, circa 1957, and two photos of their greenhouse.

To my sister Julia Ruth Claus, for photos of Aunt Gertie, Grossmama, and Pop Pop, none of which I had ever seen before, and for several photos and the original newspaper clipping of two of the Claus girls awarding the key to the City of Philadelphia to Santa Claus at the Gimbel's Thanksgiving parade, 1952.

To my sister Gretchen Yarnall, the trivia queen, for searching her family photo albums and recalling details for the stories and dates of many photos used in this book.

To my daughter, Suji Meswani, for years ago scanning lots of old family slides, and miraculously still having them on her computer so that she could quickly and easily find and send me a very special one of my maternal grandmother with her first great-grandchild, my son, Ajay, that I needed for this book.

To my son-in-law, Geoff Weiser, for scanning the photos of me and my high school boyfriend Larry from our 1961 Germantown High School yearbook, the *Revidere*.

To the late Molly Baush Hill, for slides of Analomink Lake, in the Pennsylvania Pocono Mountains, and our summer cottage there; and of my mother in a hat of her design from their trip on the Mississippi River's Delta Queen.

To Alan Berkowitz, for photos of his mother, Gisha Berkowitz.

To Howard Hill, for the photo of his late wife, Molly Baush Hill.

To Helen Kushmore Sullivan, for finding several photos of her late mother, Lillian Kushmore, from which to choose.

I cannot express my thanks strongly enough, as these photos, all unearthed in answer to my pleas, combined with ones from my own albums, give faces and bodies to the stories in this book.

To Gerardo Espinosa, of ArtPrint Express, San Miguel de Allende, Mexico, for making all of the old photos, slides, and scans sing with new life.

To Dulcie Shoener, my editor, whose meticulous and always-sensitive editing on this, our second book together, has made me a more aware and careful writer.

To Margot Boland, graphic designer, with whom I am also working on our second project together, for her creative and professional cover and book design and constant flow of good ideas for enhancement and promotion.

To all of those people—teachers, friends, fellow authors—who have helped and encouraged me to be a better writer.

Without the help of all of these people, this book would never have been published.

About the Author

Ice Cream & Pretzels is Cynthia's second book in a year. Her first book, *An Orchid Sari: The Personal Diary of an American Mom in 1960s India,* published in July 2017, recounted her nine-week trip to London and India in 1968-69 with her Indian husband and their two-year-old son.

Cynthia and her two younger sisters grew up as the daughters of two physicians in Philadelphia, Pennsylvania, the setting for most of the stories in *Ice Cream & Pretzels.* In this memoir in 17 short stories and a poem, Cynthia concentrates primarily on her childhood years in the 1940s and '50s, her parents' lives and their relationship, family dynamics, and a look back on some life-changing experiences. Vintage personal photographs of the characters and locations add texture to the narratives.

Cynthia received her B.A. degree in English from Temple University in Philadelphia.

After working for a neighborhood organizing group and at an alternative school, Cynthia served as the administrative assistant to the president for publications at The Lutheran Theological Seminary at Philadelphia for many years, being responsible for all printed materials. In that role, she was editor of the quarterly alumni/ae journal, and served as managing editor of two other journals.

After retirement, Cynthia spent 14 years as a volunteer teacher of English as a Second Language (ESL) in Philadelphia, in settings ranging from the classroom to conversation groups to one-on-one tutoring.

Since 2005, she has been an avid blogger, sharing her travel and cultural experiences, punctuated with her photographs, in places like Alaska, Morocco, South Africa, and Mexico, particularly after moving to San Miguel de Allende in 2012. For over 10 years, she has taken Spanish grammar and conversation classes. She assists Mexicans taking English classes with pronunciation and vocabulary development.

Over the years, Cynthia has taken many writing courses that resulted in short stories, some of which are in this collection. She has been and is a dedicated correspondent with dozens of friends throughout the world.

About the Typeface Used in This Book

ITC New Baskerville

History & Designers

The ITC New Baskerville™ typeface family is a modern interpretation of the original types cut in 1762 by British type founder and printer John Baskerville. During the centuries since its creation, Baskerville has remained one of the world's most widely used typefaces.

The first modern revival of Baskerville was in 1923, under the design direction of Stanley Morison for Monotype. This design was released in just two versions, roman and italic, and is still available as a digital font. In 1978, Mergenthaler Linotype Company released a revised and updated version of Baskerville that included additional weights with corresponding italics.

Through a licensing arrangement with Linotype, ITC gained the rights to the family and released ITC New Baskerville in 1982. This release made the design's roman, semi bold, bold and black weights (each with a corresponding italic) available to a much larger audience.

The original Baskerville and its revivals share design traits with old style typefaces while foreshadowing the innovations of Didot and Bodoni. As with an old style, Baskerville's serifs are heavily bracketed and its lowercase head-serifs are obliqued. Contrast in stroke weight is more pronounced than in Garamond or Caslon, yet it does not approach the extremes reached by Didot. As in a Didone, Baskerville's weight stress is vertical – gone is the inclined axis of curves found in Bembo or Centaur.

ITC New Baskerville Usage

Baskerville was created for setting books, and its modern revivals are ideally suited to the setting of continuous text. Magazines, booklets, brochures, and pamphlets are natural uses. New Baskerville is also an exceptionally legible design, with a genial, attractive feel. More than merely easy to read, New Baskerville is inviting to the reader.

Praise for *An Orchid Sari*

Praise for Cynthia Claus' first book, *An Orchid Sari: The Personal Diary of an American Mom in 1960s India,* a travel memoir published in June 2017

"An Orchid Sari is more than a travel memoir. Via her descriptive language we see, feel, smell, and taste India, a land both exotic and challenging for a young mother learning, for the first time, about her husband's birthplace. Her personal experiences engage and delight us."

Sher Davidson, author of *Europe with Two Kids and a Van* and *Under the Salvadoran Sun*

"A peek into another world, a world few of us get to see, from a woman who was an intimate part of the Indian culture. Fascinating and enlightening."

P.B. Hirschl

"Cynthia has been able to take the reader along with her through her first-hand adventures. This book is easy to read, terms are defined, and the map shows the extent of the trip. Do yourself a favor and read this book."

Barbara

"I loved the organization of the book, which began with a list

of all of the 'players,' the route, the luggage required, the hotels, and even a glossary of terms. All very helpful. The book gives you a very good sense of what it would be like to travel to a country where life is very different and to meet a whole new family, all with a two-year-old in tow."

Amazon customer

"The author skillfully tells an engaging story of her young married life and motherhood traveling among the splendors of India. I also enjoyed her candor about the inconveniences that we all encounter in other countries. Add a toddler to it and we see a bold picture of a stunning trip."

Susan Deveaux

"You really can imagine yourself there with Cynthia on her travels. It certainly makes me want to dig up my own travel diary of my year in the Middle East. This is a fun, quick read."

Amo 328

"Growing up, I had heard some stories about our family trip to India, and a few of the Ektachrome images glowed in my memory. But reading my mom's travel memoir and seeing the photos all collected in this tidy book really filled in the gaps for me and made this part of our family's history tangible and real. A true pleasure to read!"

Ajay Meswani, son of author, now age 52

"Cynthia is a truly gifted writer who lifts her readers up and takes them along on her interesting sojourn through India. What a treat to travel through the country as it was almost 50 years ago, seeing everything through the eyes of a young bride and mother meeting her Indian husband's family for the first time. Lots of interesting stories for the reader to absorb with both pathos and laughter!"

Diane

"I love a diary format, and this does not disappoint. It is both candid and exceptionally detailed, with honest emotions, the highs and lows of such a brave journey in the early 60s. I appreciated the detailed sections, explaining family members, luggage, hotels, itinerary, and more. There is also a glossary, which is both interesting and helpful. Many of the original photos, postcards, aerograms, stamps, and more were meticulously saved by the author's family members... I find the book inspires me to start to keep my own travel journals to preserve those precious memories."

Desinadora

"I admire Cynthia's journey from the perspective of a young wife and mother without prejudice, stepping outside of society's norms, embracing the adventure with her husband, traveling to meet his family, and hoping to be accepted. With her, we delight in and discover the surprises of India and family."

Ellen Ackerman, author of *Buddy's Story*

"Provides a nice peek into 1960s India and family relations and celebrations that we normal travelers don't often get to experience. A fun read."

Amazon customer

"Never judgmental, she records what must have been an overwhelming adventure with clarity, thoughtfulness, and a sense of humour. I was fascinated to watch her weave her way around an often chaotic and mysterious culture...sometimes shocked and amazed, but always remaining flexible and respectful."

Francoise Yohalem

"I got the 'insider's view' to life in 1960s India, especially through staying with family in their homes, and attending a wedding...

Felisa

"I felt like I had a peek at a different land and time without any judgments or interpretations from the author."

C. John Duey

"...her diary comments captured me. I learned many surprising facts. Cynthia Claus, through her writing, takes the reader on a journey through cultural differences. We learn of the process of adapting to the Indian culture, including the amazing primitive toilet procedure. There was one sad scene of beggars, some of them

children, contrasted by marvels of India. There was one scene with monkeys that I felt like writing a short story about. In reading An Orchid Sari, *I learned things about India I never knew and had my mind refreshed of things I had known and forgotten."*

Bill Delamar, author of *The Hidden Congregation, The Caretakers, The Brother Voice,* and *Patients in Purgatory*

"It is quite lyrical for a travelogue that spans many weeks, disparate experiences, and both joy and consternation (don't miss the toilet scene aboard an Indian train). Cynthia...projects a voice that makes so many of the experiences seem immediate and even familiar in the sense of a shared humanity with a culture very different from ours. The pictures are terrific. This is a captivating read."

Tom Ott

"We learn of the warm welcome and close connection she felt with her new relatives. She also conveys the awkwardness and peculiarities of being a 'stranger in a strange land.' Anyone who has met Cynthia in person knows that she's a candid straight-shooter, a quality that comes across in her travel diary and the aerograms sent to her family back in the U.S."

Global Citizen

"You were a great traveler: very observant and in an enviable position to see things that most travelers never get a chance to see."

Jo

"What a delightful story told in the clear, authentic voice of the author. I felt as if I was with Cynthia, as she, with very astute and often witty observations, described her first impressions of a country both exotic and challenging. The combining of diary entries and letters home made for very intimate and honest dialogue."

Agnes Olive, author of *Letters from Pakistan: One Woman's Odyssey* and *Spirit of the Earth: An Artist's Retrospective*